KNOX COLLEGE,

BY WHOM

FOUNDED AND ENDOWED;

ALSO,

A REVIEW

OF

A PAMPHLET ENTITLED

"RIGHTS OF CONGREGATIONALISTS IN KNOX COLLEGE."

BY J. W. BAILEY.

CHICAGO:
PRESS & TRIBUNE BOOK & JOB PRINTING OFFICE, 51 CLARK ST.
1860.

KNOX COLLEGE,

BY WHOM

FOUNDED AND ENDOWED;

ALSO,

A REVIEW

OF

A PAMPHLET ENTITLED

"RIGHTS OF CONGREGATIONALISTS IN KNOX COLLEGE."

BY J. W. BAILEY.

CHICAGO:
PRESS & TRIBUNE BOOK & JOB PRINTING OFFICE, 51 CLARK ST.
1860.

INTRODUCTION.

GALESBURG, ILL., July, 1859.

REV. J. W. BAILEY:

SIR: The Congregational General Association of Illinois, at their last meeting, adopted, and have since published an elaborate report, presented by a committee previously appointed, entitled "Rights of Congregationalists in Knox College." That report professes to give the results of a thorough investigation by the committee, of the facts in the case. You know, as we all know, that no such investigation was made, and that the statements of the report, taken at second-hand, are erroneous in all important particulars. Believing that such a document, if not publicly disproved, will do much injury to the College, and injustice to the Board of Trustees, we, as resident members of that Board, earnestly request you, at your earliest convenience, to prepare a full and well attested statement of the origin and endowment of Knox College, with special reference to the denominational character, and the purposes and intentions of its founders. We wish, furthermore, that you would review and expose the fallacies, and misrepresentations of the pamphlet above named, so far as a vindication of the past action of the Board, and the future interests of the College may seem to demand. By complying with this request, you will do an important service to the Institution, and confer a lasting benefit upon the community, who are interested and anxious to know the truth.

J. G. SANBURN,
S. F. DOLBEAR,
GEO. W. GALE,
N. H. LOSEY,
J. BUNCE,
H. CURTIS,
J. BULL,
SILVANUS FERRIS.

The above note sufficiently explains the reasons which led to the preparation of this pamphlet. Many things have been written of late concerning Knox College, by various parties, none of whom have based their statements upon a careful personal examination of those documents relating to the matter, which alone can be relied upon as containing the exact truth. Some have written from memory, which, however faithful it may be in presenting main facts, cannot but prove treacherous sometimes in regard to minute details. Others, including almost all who have written against the College, have been content to put in print as matters of undeniable fact, vagrant rumors and unfounded conclusions, favorable to their purpose, such as always circulate through every community which is at all agitated by the discussion of any important question. In discharging the duty imposed upon me by the Trustees of Knox College, whose names are attached to the above note, I determined upon these two things: First, to examine every book and paper belonging to the College, or to be found elsewhere, which related to its history from its origin until now. Second, to select and publish such portions of these documents as were necessary to enable the public to form for themselves an independent judgment of the nature of their testimony. In performing the first part of this labor, all the records and reports and correspondence of the original association by whom the College was founded, and of their agents and committees, have been carefully read. The records of the College, and the many reports of various committees of its Board, from its organization until the present time, have also been read. The books and the reports of the Treasurer have been examined on all the points involved in the duty assigned me. The records of the First Presbyterian Church in Galesburg, which was the first Church established here, have been read with great care, from the time the first meetings were held with reference to an organization, down to the last year. Much miscellaneous matter, bearing upon the history of the College, has also received an attentive perusal. In all this labor, the sole object has been to make myself personally familiar with all the facts which I desired to present to the public, and thus to escape the charge of having narrated anything important upon second-hand testimony. I have first examined the documents upon which all my statements are based in every instance, and then have given these documents to the public that they may test the accuracy of my statements. Only in this way can the public be sure that they are not misled. It is not individual opinions upon controverted points that is asked for by those interested in this matter, so much as the facts upon which all correct opinions must be based. With the facts in their possession, all can form their own opinions. Without these, the public must always remain in uncertainty, especially when opinions are divided.

INTRODUCTION.

The publication of the pamphlet has been delayed beyond the time when it was first promised. This has arisen from the pressure of other duties, and from the amount of labor involved in such an examination as I had undertaken, which has been much greater than any one can imagine who has never been engaged in a similar work. The pamphlet is now sent forth to the public with the earnest desire that it may prove instrumental in correcting the many errors which have of late been widely circulated concerning the College. That man is not to be envied who can take pleasure in doing injury to such an institution as Knox College. The extraordinary efforts to impair its usefulness which have been made of late by more persons than one, indicate a state of feeling on this subject which cannot be regarded as praiseworthy. The Colleges of the State of Illinois are among its chief agencies for securing the highest prosperity of the people. Whoever injures them commits a great wrong against the whole State. The public will not fail to hold to a strict accountability, any man, or any class of men, who for selfish ends decry and misrepresent and seriously injure their Colleges.

J. W. BAILEY.

GALESBURG, ILL., March, 1860.

The undersigned, Secretary and Treasurer of the Board of Trust of Knox College, have examined carefully all the references to, and extracts from, the records and other documents in our possession, made by Rev. J. W. BAILEY, in a pamphlet entitled "Knox College, etc., etc.," and we hereby certify that such references and extracts are strictly correct.

S. F. DOLBEAR,
Secretary of the Board of Trust.

O. S. PITCHER,
Treasurer.

KNOX COLLEGE.

ITS ORIGIN.

Knox College, in Galesburg, Illinois, was founded on the 7th day of January, in the year 1836, by a number of persons then living in the State of New York, who were associated together as Subscribers to a Plan for establishing literary institutions in the West. Those Subscribers met on that day, in Whitesboro', N. Y., and there, in accordance with their Plan, organized the College, appointed its Board of Trustees, and then donated to it several thousand acres of land lying in Illinois, where Galesburg now is, which they had purchased solely as an endowment for the College. The sale of these lands has furnished nearly all the money which has been required to meet the current expenses of the Institution, including the College proper, an Academy, a Preparatory Department, and a Female Seminary, and also to erect large and costly buildings; and which has so enriched its treasury that it is now one of the wealthiest Colleges in our land. The present noble endowment of this College has been derived almost wholly from the liberality of its founders.

The credit of the whole enterprise is due in the first instance to the Rev. George W. Gale, D. D., a Presbyterian, from whom the Plan, in all its details, originated, and to whose persevering efforts and many personal sacrifices it owed its consummation. His Plan, in its main features, was to secure by subscription, money enough to purchase in some desirable location in the Western States, government land to the amount of one township, or thirty-six square miles. Out of this land when purchased, enough was to be reserved for the site of a village, and also of the College which was to be organized. The remainder of the land was to be divided into farms of convenient size, and appraised at an average value of five dollars an acre, which would be just four times the amount paid for it. At this increased valuation, the Subscribers were to be allowed to take farming lands to the amount of their subscription. The remainder was to be donated to the College. The village property was also to be divided into suitable building lots, and sold only to actual settlers. The money thus obtained was to be appropriated to an Academy and a Young Ladies' Seminary, so far as needed, and the remainder to the College. The Circular and details of the Plan are here published, and deserve the attentive perusal of the reader, as they show the enlarged views of Mr. Gale and of those who engaged with him in founding the College, and that the enterprise was one of pure Christian benevolence.

CIRCULAR AND PLAN.

"The indications of Providence, as well as the requisitions of Christ, impose on Christians of this day peculiar obligations to devise and execute, as far as in them lies, liberal and efficient plans for spreading the gospel through the world. The supply of an evangelical and able ministry, is in the whole circle of means, confessedly the most important for the accomplishment of this end: all other means are the mere aids and implements of the living preacher. And yet, important as it is to the sustaining of the church, and the conversion of the world, there is reason to believe that the business of furnishing a devoted and efficient ministry, has entered less into the calculations of Christians at large, than any other department of benevolent effort of the present day; certainly much less in proportion to its magnitude. Perhaps they have thought this a work peculiarly the Lord's, in which they had very little to do. But the language of our Saviour, 'Pray ye the Lord of the harvest to send forth laborers,' and the fact that they are to be furnished, not by miracle, but by the slow process of education, prove, that we have *much* to do; especially when we look at the field which our own country, to say nothing of the wide world, spreads out before us; a field 'white for the harvest.'

Who that loves the souls of men can look on this field and not feel his heart affected, and not tax his energies to the utmost, as well as offer his most fervent prayers to the Lord of the harvest, that he would furnish the laborers? Who that loves the institutions of his country, can look upon it without alarm, when he reflects that in a few, a *very* few years, they will be in the hands of a population reared in this field; and reared, unless a mighty effort be made by evangelical Christians, under the forming hand of those who are no less the enemies of civil liberty, than of a pure gospel? What is done to prevent this ruin must be done quickly. It is perfectly within the power of evangelical Christians in this country, under God, to furnish, and that speedily, all the laborers wanted on this field, besides doing much towards supplying the world. The men are already furnished; if not, 'the Lord of the harvest' *will* furnish them. Hundreds of youth of talent, and piety, and enterprise, stand ready to enter upon the work of preparation, whenever a 'wide and effectual door is opened' for them. The manual labor system, if properly sustained and conducted, will open to them that door. It is peculiarly adapted not only to qualify men for the self-denying and arduous duties of the gospel ministry, especially in our new settlements and missionary fields abroad, but to call them out; to induce them to enter upon the work of preparation. It is an important fact that while other institutions are many of them, greatly in want of students, these, with all the disadvantages under which they have to labor, are not only filled, but great numbers are rejected for want of means to accommodate them. Let institutions be established on this plan, having all the requisitions and facilities for profitable labor, in connection with the advantages for literary acquisitions enjoyed in our well endowed seminaries, and there will be no lack of students; especially if there be added to these the means of gratuitous instruction to the indigent. Let such provision be made, and three-fourths of the indigent young men will ask no other aid; and should they ask it, the church would do them a favor to refuse them, and leave them to their efforts to make up the deficiency.

It is beginning to be believed, and not without good reason, that females are to act a much more important part in the conversion of the world, than has been generally supposed; not as preachers of the gospel, but as help-meets of those who are; and as instructors and guides of the rising generation, not only in the nursery, but in the public school: it should therefore be an object of special aim with all who pray and labor for the conversion of the world, to provide for the thorough and well directed education of females. Experiment has already proved, that manual labor may be successfully introduced into Female Seminaries, and that it is highly conducive to health and piety, and adapted to reduce the expenses of education, sufficiently to encourage many young ladies to qualify themselves in such seminaries for fields of usefulness, who, without that encouragement would never have put forth such efforts. What has been done on this subject shows the importance, and proves the feasibility of doing much more. It is perfectly in the power of *a few families of moderate property* to rear up such institutions, at this time, in the valley of the Mississippi, on a permanent basis, *with a great part of the endowment required*, and on a liberal and extensive scale, with great advantage to themselves and families. Such a plan is here proposed, with the design, if it may please the Lord, to carry it into effect.

PLAN.

Let a subscription be opened for such Institutions in some part of the valley to be fixed upon by a majority of the Subscribers, and when $40,000 shall have been raised, let those who propose to settle in the vicinity of the Institutions meet and elect a Board of Trustees, who shall have charge of all the funds, the appointment of officers, and perform other duties usually belonging to trustees of literary institutions. Let a committee also be appointed by the Subscribers, to locate the Institutions, and make a purchase of land under such instructions as shall be given them.

2. Let a tract or tracts of land be purchased equal in quantity at least, to a town six miles square, at the government price, if it can be so obtained, and let this land, or so much of it as may be wanted by the Subscribers, be appraised at five dollars an acre, on an average; every Subscriber who shall purchase eighty acres, or half a quarter-section, to be paid for by the money subscribed, shall be entitled to the gratuitous instruction of one youth in the College, Preparatory School, or Female Seminary, for *twenty-five* years, which right may be used, rented, or sold at his pleasure. The same privilege shall be attached to every eighty acres thus purchased by original Subscribers.

3. After paying for the land, the remainder of the fund of 40,000 dollars, and as much more as the Board of Trustees may judge expedient, shall be expended as soon as practicable in the erection of College edifices. The title of all land not deeded to the original settlers, shall be vested in the Board of Trustees. Mill-seats in the tract shall be at their disposal for the benefit of the College fund.

4. Three contiguous sections, of 640 acres, shall be reserved for the purposes of the College and the village, to be appropriated as the Board shall order. The village shall be laid out into lots by a committee appointed by the Subscribers, and appraised in a manner similar to the farms. Those who choose may have a lot, or lots in the village at the same rate that the quarter sections of land are appraised on average, with the same right of gratuitous education attached.

5. All the land purchased, except that of the village, after supplying the original Subscribers, shall be sold or rented, as the Board may deem best, for the interest of the College. Out of this land and such other money as may be obtained, a fund of 50,000 dollars should be set apart in scholarships of 400 dollars each, as a permanent fund, the interest of which shall be applied to defray the expense of tuition and room rent for pious and indigent young men who have the ministry in view.

The money arising from village lots shall constitute a fund for the erection of a Female Seminary, and Academy, or a preparatory school for male youth, and for the support of teachers. If the fund amount to more than 50,000 dollars, it *may* be applied to the support of the College.

6. The College to be established shall be on the manual labor plan, every pupil being required to labor not more than three, nor less than two hours a day on the farm, in the garden, or in mechanic shops. The course of study shall be liberal and thorough; the Bible, in the original tongue, shall be made a class book; and among others, there shall be a professor who shall perform the spe-

cial duties of a pastor to the students connected with the College and preparatory school.

7. The Female Seminary shall be under the care of a gentleman, as principal, who shall have the general management and spiritual instruction of the pupils. The immediate government and literary instruction shall chiefly be committed to ladies. The Institution shall be of a high order as it respects instruction, and adapted to give such an education as an intelligent Christian parent would wish; and the instruction so directed as to qualify the pupils for the business of instructing, or for missionary or domestic life. The preservation of health by systematic exercise shall receive special attention. Manual labor, so far as it may be desired by the parent, or necessary to reduce expense for the encouragement of indigent pupils, shall be incorporated with it.

8. A Theological Seminary, and Medical School, shall be established in connection with the College as soon as it shall be thought best by the Board, and funds can be raised.

9. One half of the subscription money shall be payable when the sum proposed of 40,000 dollars shall have been subscribed by responsible persons; and the other half in one year after, with interest from the time the first instalment is due; a note being given for the same to the Board of Trustees.

10. These articles may be amended or altered by the Subscribers comprehended in the original subscription of $40,000 whenever a majority of them shall think best; provided no right of property is infringed, and the essential constitution and design of the literary institutions are not changed thereby."

With this plan Mr. Gale went almost exclusively among those of his personal friends who were connected with Presbyterian churches in Central and Eastern New York, and solicited their coöperation in his work. In the early part of the year 1835, he had secured subscriptions to the amount of about twenty-one thousand dollars.[*] Although this was only a little more than one-half the amount required to be raised by the plan, yet it was thought best, by those most interested, to call a meeting of the Subscribers at this time, in order to organize and send out at once a Committee of Exploration. That meeting was held on the sixth day of May, 1835, at Rome, New York. The minutes of that meeting and of all subsequent meetings of the Subscribers to Mr. Gale's plan, are entered

---

[*] In addition to this several persons, *not* Subscribers, agreed *to loan* the Association a few thousand dollars if it should be needed. This money was to be paid back, with interest, as soon as possible. *The money was never required* by the Association. In a statement made two years ago, by parties connected with the College, this sum was added to that pledged by the Subscribers, and the total given at about $28,000, without indicating that a part was pledged by persons who were not Subscribers, and pledged only as a loan. The whole sum pledged by Subscribers was, as stated above, only about $21,000.

in the first volume of the College Records, and are all recorded as having been approved by the Board of Trustees after the College was founded. The following are the minutes of the

FIRST MEETING OF THE SUBSCRIBERS.

" At a meeting of the Subscribers to the Circular of G. W. Gale, proposing to establish a literary institution in the Valley of the Mississippi, (see plan annexed to the previous page) held at the session-room of the 1st Presbyterian Church, in Rome, on Wednesday, May 6, 1835, the following proceedings were had:

After spending a season in prayer, the meeting was called to order by the appointment of the Rev. John Waters, Chairman, and T. B. Jervis, Secretary.

On motion of Rev. Mr. Gale,

Resolved, That a committee be chosen to nominate a Prudential Committee.

Resolved, That the Nominating Committee consist of Rev. Mr. Kellogg, Rev. Mr. Gale and Mr. Holt.

On motion of Rev. Mr. Kellogg,

Resolved, That Messrs. Blodget, T. B. Jervis and Stedman, be appointed a committee to bring before the meeting in the afternoon such topics of discussion as, in their opinion, should engage the attention of the meeting.

Adjourned to 2 o'clock P. M.

At 2 o'clock the meeting convened according to adjournment. The Committee of Nomination reported that they recommend that the Prudential Committee should not exceed eleven, and the following persons as members, with power to fill vacancies, viz: Walter Webb, Adams; Nehemiah West, Ira; Thomas Gilbert, Rome; John C. Smith, Utica; G. W. Gale, Whitesboro'; H. H. Kellogg, Clinton.

The report was accepted and adopted.

Resolved, That the Prudential Committee procure the exploration of the country lying in the States of Indiana and Illinois, between the 40th and 42nd degrees of north latitude, with reference to selecting the best location in the district for the projected literary Institution.

Resolved, That an Exploring Committee of three be appointed by the Prudential Committee.

Resolved, That the Prudential Committee be authorized to assume the expense that has been incurred, and also that which it is necessary to incur in raising the fund of forty thousand dollars.

Resolved, That the Prudential Committee be authorized to incur such expense as may be necessary to accomplish the objects of their appointment.

Resolved, That the Prudential Committee be instructed *to call a*

meeting of the Subscribers to the fund, as soon as they shall be able to communicate such information as in their view is necessary to enable the Subscribers to instruct a Purchasing Committee.

T. B. JERVIS, *Sec'y*."

On the same day on which they were appointed, the Prudential Committee met and organized, and then, according to their instructions, appointed an Exploring Committee, consisting of Nehemiah West, Thomas Gilbert, and Timothy B. Jervis. They also appointed Rev. G. W. Gale a general agent of the Association, formed by the Subscribers.

The agent and all the members of both the above committees were Presbyterians.

The minutes of this meeting of the Prudential Committee are on file with the Secretary of the College, the main items of which are as follows:

"May 6th, 1835. The Prudential Committee of the New York Society, for Establishing a Settlement, College, &c., in the Valley of the Mississippi, met at the house of the Rev. Mr. Sedgwick, at Rome, according to appointment. Nehemiah West and Thomas Gilbert were appointed an Exploring Committee to examine all the important points for effecting the objects of the Society in the North of the States of Indiana and Illinois, according to the instructions suggested by the Society at their meeting this day. Rev. Geo. W. Gale was appointed a general agent to procure families and funds, with a salary of $700 a year, and his necessary expenses, to be borne by the Society. There being no other individual present or known to the Committee, (as the third member of the Exploring Committee,) the Secretary was instructed to correspond with gentlemen and report at the next meeting. Timothy B. Jervis was chosen a member of the Prudential Committee. Adjourned to meet in Whitesboro', May the 12th, 1835, at the house of the Rev. G. W. Gale."

"Whitesboro', May 12, 1835. Prudential Committee met according to adjournment. Mr. Gale reported that he had made inquiries by letter and otherwise, but had not been able to ascertain definitely whether any of the gentlemen he had in view would accept an appointment as one of the Exploring Committee. After some deliberation and consultation with Mr. Jervis, a member of the Prudential Committee, it was resolved unanimously to appoint him."

The three gentlemen above named accepted their appointment as an Exploring Committee, and immediately proceeded west in discharge of the duties assigned them. Nearly three months were spent by them in exploring portions of Indiana and Illinois. They early experienced a difficulty growing out of that part of the plan of the Association which required the purchase of a whole township of government land. It was not easy at that time to find thirty-six square miles of land, all subject to entry at government price, which would combine fertility, and healthfulness, and desirableness of location, such as would render it a proper site for a colony and a College. This committee, in their correspondence with the Prudential Committee, which is on file with the Secretary of the College, clearly stated the difficulty, and also urgently pressed the importance of securing a modification of the original plan, so far as to allow the purchase of a less amount of land than was at first proposed. If the Association would consent to such a change of their plan, the committee were prepared, from the survey they had made, to recommend "the Military Tract," in Illinois, as the region which would "afford altogether the best opportunity for" accomplishing the purposes of their appointment. At a later date the Prudential Committee were informed that "Mr. Gilbert had found a township on the Military Tract which he thought would answer" as a site for the College. This township was the one adjoining the south-east corner of that within which the Association afterward planted their College. Mr. Jervis recommended, in addition to the proposed change in the plan, that a Purchasing Committee should be appointed at once. In his letter he thus writes: "I can give you no idea of the flood of immigration that is pouring into this region of the West this season, and I would earnestly press the importance of the Purchasing Committee leaving you by the middle of August, and of the funds necessary to purchase the land being placed to their credit as early as September. Now is most emphatically the time for the friends of Zion to come up to the work of giving the means of intellectual and moral instruction to the inhabitants of the great valley."

The Prudential Committee, having become well satisfied, from the letters of the Exploring Committee, that a whole township of government land could not be found in such a region as they desired, but that enough to accomplish all the objects of the Association could be secured upon the "Military Tract," in Illinois, called the Subscribers together in a second meeting, which was held on the 19th day of August, 1835, at Whitesboro', New York. At this meeting the original plan was modified so far as to authorize the purchase of twenty instead of thirty-six sections of land. A Purchasing Committee was also appointed, consisting of Rev. G. W. Gale, Silvanus

Ferris and Nehemiah West. These gentlemen were all Presbyterians. The following are the minutes of that

SECOND MEETING OF SUBSCRIBERS.

"At a meeting of the Subscribers to Rev. G. W. Gale's Circular, proposing the erection of a College in the Valley of the Mississippi, held at Whitesboro', August 19, 1835, Mr. S. Bond, of Adams, was chosen Chairman, and I. Holt, of Watertown, Secretary.

The forenoon was spent in prayer and other religious exercises, and in the afternoon the following resolutions were adopted:

Resolved, That a committee of three persons be appointed to make a purchase and appraisal of lands in Illinois or Indiana, *for the objects specified in the circular*, and that G. W. Gale, H. H. Kellogg and Silvanus Ferris be that committee; also, that Nehemiah West be a substitute for Mr. Kellogg.

Resolved, That those who visit the land this coming fall, with a view to remove their families at furthest in the spring, have their choice of lots, at the appraisal of the Purchasing Committee.

Resolved, That *the distribution* of lots to Subscribers who do not go on this fall and make choice under the preceding resolution, shall be deferred until a meeting of the Subscribers the coming winter.

Resolved, That the Purchasing Committee give such security for monies received of the Subscribers, as the Prudential Committee deem safe.

Resolved, That it is inexpedient to purchase less than twenty sections, and as much more as the committee have funds to appropriate.

Resolved, That if necessary, the location of timber-land separate from prairie, in the purchase, shall not constitute an obstacle to the prosecution of our plan.

Resolved, That timber-land be put at the average price of prairie, and that one-tenth of the purchase be timber, and Subscribers, if they require it, be furnished with timber in that proportion.

Adjourned."

The reader will take notice that by their action in this second meeting, the Subscribers bound themselves to meet all the cost of the twenty sections of land when purchased: The Purchasing Committee were acting under their instructions and as their agents merely. In order to purchase the amount of land required, and to meet other expenses, the committee would need somewhat more than sixteen thousand dollars. By the terms of the original subscription, the money subscribed was *not yet due*, and although a Purchasing Committee had now been appointed, yet the Subscribers were not all able to advance at once the amount to be paid by them. A few of them, however, paid their subscription at that time, amounting in all to somewhat less than five thousand dollars. To this was added the proceeds of a note of eight hundred dollars given by Mr. R. N. Randall, of Whitesboro', a Presbyterian, who was not a Subscriber, but who had pledged what aid he could give to the enterprise. The Treasury Books of Knox College contain the names of the persons who paid this money, and the amount paid by each one, in the following entry:

Purchasing Committee, Dr., to Trustees of Knox College, for money received, Oct. 1, 1835,

Of R. N. Randall	$ 781 75
" G. W. Gale	1,194 11
" H. H. Kellogg	1,000 00
" Gurdon Grant	400 00
" John Waters	1,000 00
" S. Ferris	400 00
" T. Simmons	300 00
" J. Frost	200 00
Total	$5,275 86

In addition to this amount, other Subscribers agreed to advance the sum of nearly two thousand dollars, which, however, was not received by the committee in time for their use, as appears from the agent's report, which will be given in its proper place.

An additional sum of ten thousand dollars was advanced as a loan by Messrs. Gale and Ferris, two members of the Purchasing Committee. This money they obtained on their joint note, made payable at the Bank of Utica in four months from date. By an arrangement with the bank the money on this note was drawn from the Bank of Michigan, at Detroit. The Purchasing Committee were thus provided with money, which, after deducting exchange and discount, amounted to fifteen thousand and ninety-four dollars and eighty-four cents. As the duties of this committee were important and arduous, they desired, before they left for the West, an increase of their number. After some inquiry, it was ascertained that Mr. Thomas Simmons, one of the Subscribers, would be willing to accompany them, and accordingly he was appointed one of the Purchasing Committee. He received his appointment from the Prudential Committee. Mr. Simmons was a Congregationalist, and was the only one, among the thirty-four Subscribers, by whom Knox College was founded, who belonged to that denomination. The amount of his subscription was eight hundred dollars, of which only three hundred were now advanced by him toward purchasing the land; the remainder was paid at a later date.

Messrs. Gale, Ferris and West left in company for the "Military Tract," in Illinois, on the 16th day of September, 1835. At Detroit they were joined by Mr. Simmons. Here they drew from the Bank of Michigan the money on the note of ten thousand dollars, given by Mr. Gale and Mr. Ferris. Mr. Gale had been taken seriously ill before reaching Detroit, and was unable to proceed further. The other members of the committee left that city on the 29th of September, intending to proceed to Knoxville, in Knox county, Illinois, where they had been directed by the previous Exploring Committee. On their way they spent two days at Ottawa, and while there were joined by Mr. Samuel Tompkins, a neighbor of Mr. Simmons. The two had travelled in company from their home, in Hamilton, New York, to Detroit, where they had separated. Mr. Tompkins was an humble mechanic, a shoemaker, of such limited means that he had travelled principally on foot from Detroit to Ottawa, looking for a new home for himself in the great West. At this point he was engaged by the committee to go on to Knoxville, and there assist them in surveying the land which they were about to purchase. The compensation to be allowed him was his travelling expenses, and no more, from Ottawa to Knoxville, and thence to his home in New York. The committee, having secured his services, then left him to follow them, as he did, on foot. He afterward rendered them faithful service in carrying the chain for the surveyors. His only connection with the committee was that of a hired assistant. These facts respecting him are stated upon the authority of Mr. S. Ferris, the principal member of the committee, and his son, Mr. S. Weston Ferris, who accompanied them through their whole journey. Mr. Tompkins was a Congregationalist. He was never a Subscriber to the Plan of founding Knox College, and until after the College was founded, had never had any connection with the enterprise, except that of having been employed by the Purchasing Committee to carry the chain for their surveyors. Among all the records, and reports and documents of various kinds relating to the founding of the College, his name never appears except in the bill of expenses of the Purchasing Committee, who report him as having received $52.75.

In the report of the Purchasing Committee, a portion of which will soon be given, this language occurs in narrating the action of the committee in purchasing the lands in Knox county: "On the 30th of October *two* of your committee left the tract and returned to Quincy, to complete their entry, and the *other* returned directly home." The two who went to Quincy were Messrs. Ferris and West—the "other" was Mr. Simmons. This shows that the committee did not regard Mr. Tompkins, who was then with them, as one of their number. Yet in the face of these facts, so anxious has Mr. Blanchard, the Ex-President of the College, been to establish the "rights of Congregationalists" to its control, that from want of any better foundation, he has on several different occasions publicly advanced Mr. Tompkins as the principal actor in purchasing the lands and as the main founder of the College. His argument has always rested upon the fact that Mr. Tompkins was with the Purchasing Committee when they bought the lands for the Association; but he appears never to have known, or if he did know he never saw fit to tell the public what the true relations were between Mr. Tompkins and that committee. Mr. Tompkins, who now lives in Galesburg, must have been immeasurably surprised to learn, through Mr. Blanchard, how much the world owes to him as the chief founder of Knox College.

The committee left Ottawa on the 12th of October, and proceeded to Knox county, upon the "Military Tract." Here they soon found, as they had been led to expect, from the correspondence of the Exploring Committee, a site in every respect suited to their purposes.

They immediately expended their funds in purchasing $10,746 \frac{81}{100}$ acres, or about seventeen sections of land. In this amount were included two improved farms of 250 acres, and 160 acres of timber land, all of which cost $1,900. The remaining $10,336 \frac{81}{100}$ acres consisted of most beautiful and fertile prairie land, not dotted by any human habitation, and which cost, at government price, $12,921.01. The total cost of all the land was ($14,821.01) fourteen thousand eight hundred and twenty-one dollars, and one cent. The two improved farms and the quarter-section of timber land were purchased in the name of the whole Committee, Messrs. Ferris, West, Gale and Simmons; but the remainder was all purchased in the name of Mr. Ferris and of Mr. West. If Mr. Tompkins had been a member of the committee, his name would have been inserted in those first deeds. The committee surveyed the land, selected a site for the village, and also for the College, and agreed to call the town Galesburg, after the author of the whole enterprise. They then, in the early part of November, 1835, left for their homes in New York. A meeting of the Subscribers was called to receive their report, to take possession of the land, and to found the College. That meeting was held on the 7th day of January, 1836, at Whitesboro',

New York. At that meeting the Subscribers assumed the entire ownership of the land; they founded the College, calling it "Prairie College;" they determined the number that should constitute the Board; they elected ten Trustees to act as a *quasi* corporation until a charter could be obtained; they required the Purchasing Committee to give bonds for the proper conveyance of the land to the Trustees of the College for its benefit; they gave the name of Galesburg to their prospective town; and they then, according to the plan to which they had subscribed, took farm lands of the Association at an average price four times greater than that at which they had just been bought of the government. This they did in order to insure the immediate success of their plan. The College was *founded* at this meeting. These *Subscribers*, and they only, were its *founders*. They had originated a plan for founding the College; they had purchased thousands of acres of land in order to endow it; they then organized it by name; they appointed its Board of Trustees; they vested the title to the land in its Board; and, finally, many of them gave themselves as colonists, forsaking pleasant homes in the East and consenting to endure the privations of western pioneer life, in order to insure the most perfect success to their undertaking. The land which they then gave as an endowment to their College has, in the few years since that time, been worth to it more than HALF A MILLION OF DOLLARS.

The reader is asked to compare the acts of these Subscribers in founding Knox College, with the acts of the ten ministers who founded Yale College, and whose claim as founders was maintained and established by President Clapp, when disputed in 1763, before the Governor and Council of the Colony of Connecticut. President Woolsey, in a "Historical Discourse," delivered in 1850, thus speaks of the manner of founding Yale College: "Some time in the year 1700, ten ministers, acting by general consent for the ministry and the churches of the colony of Connecticut, held a meeting at New Haven, for the purpose of founding a Collegiate School; and this purpose they carried into effect at a subsequent meeting at Branford, in the same year, when each person *presented a number of books* to the body, using words to this effect as he laid the books on the table: 'I give these books for the founding of a College in this colony.'" "*The act of founding* consisted in their giving *forty folios* for the purpose of establishing a College in the colony." "The ten ministers who met at Branford in 1700, being a society, and a quasi-corporation by nomination and consent of a body of ministers and people, and having made a donation to the College, as well as received property in trust for it *before* the charter, were in reality its founders by the common law, and thus had the right of visitation which they transmitted to their legal successors." If these ten ministers, who donated forty folios, were thus the founders of Yale College, then, beyond all question, the thirty-four Subscribers, who, in addition to all their other acts to the same effect, donated thousands of acres of land to establish and endow Knox College, were its founders. The following are the minutes of the meeting of the Subscribers when the College was founded:

THIRD MEETING OF SUBSCRIBERS.

"At a meeting of the Subscribers to the Circular of the Rev. G. W. Gale, for the purchase of lands on which to locate a College, etc., in the Valley of the Mississippi, held at Whitesboro', on the 7th January, 1836, John Waters was elected Chairman, and N. H. Losey Secretary. The session was opened with prayer by Rev. Ira Pettibone. Minutes of last meeting were read. Report of the agent, G. W. Gale, was accepted."

As the several reports presented at this meeting, are long and would occupy too much space in this pamphlet, if published entire, it is necessary to present only such portions of them as relate directly to the facts already stated. These reports are valuable documents, in which may be found almost the entire history of the founding of the College. The following statements are taken from the above mentioned Agent's Report:

"It will be recollected by those who attended our meeting to appoint a Purchasing Committee, that Mr. Silvanus Ferris, Rev. H. H. Kellogg, and myself, were appointed for that purpose, with instructions to collect funds and purchase, if possible, twenty sections of land. It being doubtful whether Mr. Kellogg would be able to go, at his suggestion Mr. West, who had been out as one of the Exploring Committee, was appointed in his stead. The Prudential Committee, feeling that it was very important to have a full committee, and some of the committee feeling that the duties would be arduous as well as highly responsible, thought best to appoint Mr. T. Simmons, of Hamilton, in addition. There was one place on the Military Tract, in Knox county, which Mr. Gilbert had seen, and in which he had purchased, which he thought would do, and which was nearly all Congress land. A consultation was held by the committee and some friends, as to what was expedient to be done. A few advanced what funds they could. We raised between 5,000 and 6,000 dollars, and made arrangements for more, but in some of it we were disappointed, and some that was sent on did not reach the committee in time. The committee also resolved to effect a loan through the Bank, if possible, which they did on their own responsibility, of $10,000. This they supposed would enable them nearly or quite to meet the wishes and instructions of the Subscribers in the amount of land to be purchased, which it did nearly, and would have done quite, but for the disappointment just mentioned. Mr. Simmons arrived soon after the rest of the committee did, at Detroit. I would add that our list of Subscribers amounts to forty-six. There were a few who subscribed, but who, discouraged about our making a purchase, have settled in Michigan."

"Report of Prudential Committee was read by its chairman, H. H. Kellogg and accepted."

(The following are among its statements:)

"The doings of this committee *were reported to this body at their last meeting.* They then stated that an Exploring Committee had been sent out, one of whom, as was expected, had returned and was then present. Mr. Gilbert had found a township on the Military Tract which he thought would answer, and after deliberation, it was thought best to get what money could be obtained, and to send out the Committee. This was done as reported by the agent. The amount of money expended in land and the expense attending the purchase, will be reported by the Purchasing Committee. The committee would now recommend that the lots should be distributed in the way the Subscribers may think best, and that trustees be chosen to make conveyance of property to Subscribers, after receiving it from the committee, and to take charge of all the business relating to the College, and other literary institutions. The business for which the Prudential Committee were appointed having been accomplished, they now tender their resignation."

"Report of the Purchasing Committee was read by Mr. West, and accepted." [This report is very long, but only the following facts of all which it contains need be now published:] "On examining the tract in Illinois, they (the committee) found that it combined more desirable objects than they had heretofore expected to find. They found it delightfully situated on the height of land, and nearly central between the two rivers, beautifully watered with living springs and streams, and having an abundance of coal and building stone, and unquestionably healthful. Accordingly they decided at once to plant their feet there, and commenced making the purchase. In the first place they purchased two improved farms, the one containing 150, the other 100 acres, for $1,500. They also bought one quarter-section of timber, adjoining the first purchase, for $2.50 per acre ($400.) They then left immediately for Quincy, a distance of one hundred miles, where the land office is kept, to make entries of what prairie land was needed. The whole amount of funds belonging to the company invested was $15,094.84. The quantity of land purchased is, 410 acres of resident individuals, and 10,336 $\frac{81}{100}$ acres of the government, making the whole purchase amount to 10,746 $\frac{81}{100}$ acres. In addition to the above purchase, your committee invested private funds sufficient to secure the remainder of the township, so that now it will be entirely under the control of the colony, a circumstance highly favorable to our mutual improvement. Thus, we have given briefly the outlines of our expedition and success. Should the blessing of Heaven attend our labors, and we succeed in raising up a seminary of learning in the great valley, and thus be instrumental in sending the Bread of Life to those that are ready to perish, multitudes in the realms of glory may yet rise up and call us blessed. Your committee would recommend that this meeting proceed immediately *to divide* the land among the Subscribers, agreeably to the original plan, and that we elect nine Trustees, who shall have the charge of all the property, landed or otherwise, belonging to the Institution, and who shall, as soon as practicable, be incorporated by the Legislature of the State of Illinois, by the name of the 'Trustees of Prairie College, Ill.'

Monies received by Purchasing Committee........$15,094 84

Amount of purchase, 10,746 $\frac{81}{100}$ acres.............$14,821 01
Expenses paid by Mr. Ferris..................... 636 20
Exploring Committee.......................... 517 41
(Agent) 584 45

$16,559 07

The plan of *distributing lots to Subscribers* was referred to a committee of three, also the continuance of scholarships, and mode of conveyance, and Messrs. J. C. Smith, Silvanus Ferris, and Thomas Simmons, were appointed that committee.

Resolved, That we proceed to appoint a BOARD OF TRUSTEES, *agreeably to the plan to which we subscribed*, and that the number of which the Board shall consist, and the nomination of the Board, be referred to a committee.

Messrs. Gale, Kellogg and West were appointed that committee.

Resolved, That a committee of three be appointed to report what is to be done for the improvement of the public lands, a name for the College and village, and what, if anything, shall be done to guard the morals of the colony.

Messrs. Smith, West and Tompkins were appointed that committee. Adjourned to meet again at 2 o'clock P. M.

2 o'clock P. M. Met according to adjournment. The Committee of nomination, etc., made the following Report: That the Board consist of twenty-five, when full; that it is now inexpedient to fill it; and nominate as trustees the following persons: John Waters, Silvanus Ferris, H. H. Kellogg, Thos. Simmons, Samuel Bond, John C. Smith and Walter Webb. The report was accepted and adopted.

Mr. Bond requested that his name be stricken out, which was granted, and G. W. Gale and Nehemiah West were nominated and appointed.

Isaac Mills and Samuel Tompkins were also appointed.

The committee to whom the plan of distributing, etc., was referred, reported, That lots as appraised, *be received on subscription*—choice or preference be decided by *bid*—bids for general fund—80 acres, at any price, entitled to scholarships—and that to future purchasers, until scholarships amount to eighty if taken in sixty days, lots shall be entitled to scholarships, and in other cases, at the discretion of the trustees—that the Purchasing Committee be requested to hold the duplicates, and give bonds for the due conveyance, so soon as circumstances will admit, agreeably to the original plan, to the trustees, and in the mean time, certificates or deeds to purchasers, when directed by the trustees. The report was accepted and adopted.

Resolved, That if any one becomes dissatisfied with his choice of a lot, and wishes to exchange with the trustees, for lots in their possession, designed for settlers, he may have the privilege at the appraisal.

Resolved, That the agent be directed to designate individuals to select lots for absent subscribers who have requested it.

Resolved, That we proceed to the distribution of lots. See memorandum of sales file No. 4, also treasurer's books.

The committee to whom was referred the plan of improving public lands, etc., reported,

That the village be immediately laid out under the direction of the trustees, appraised and thrown into market:

That lots for an academy or preparatory school, ladies seminary, meeting house and common school, and for other benevolent objects, as the trustees may deem expedient, be reserved from the village tract:

That arrangements be made by the trustees, for cultivating and fencing the College land the present year; also for *procuring material for a College edifice,* so that it be commenced as early as the spring of 1837:

That provision be made for the *erection of a steam saw-mill*, either from the public fund or private enterprise, giving preference to the latter:

That the College be named Prairie College, and the village Galesburg:

That *a house be built* at the earliest practicable period, by the trustees, for boarding and entertainment:

That the trustees *furnish wood land* for each purchaser who requires it, equal to one-tenth of their purchase; which report was accepted and adopted.

In the course of the meeting, Mr. Losey resigned the office of Secretary, and J. C. Smith was appointed in his room.

JNO. C. SMITH, *Sec'y.*

The foregoing records were approved by the board.

J. C. SMITH, *Sec'y.*"

The reader has not failed to notice from the foregoing minutes, that the persons who held the several meetings recorded, invariably style themselves "the Subscribers to the Circular of Rev. G. W. Gale for founding literary institutions"—that in the reports of the several committees similar language is used in designating those by whom they were appointed—that the Prudential Committee, which was appointed at the first meeting of the Subscribers, presented a report at the second, and again at the third meeting, and at the last meeting tendered their resignation—that the agent also, who was appointed at the first meeting, reported at the last—that all the transactions, from the first to the last meeting, were an uninterrupted series, ending in the accomplishment of the original plan—and that from first to last the "Subscribers," and they only, were the responsible parties engaged in the work, and by whom the College was founded.

Those readers who live in Galesburg and vicinity, and who heard Ex-President Blanchard, when he introduced himself upon the platform after the inaugural address of his successor, a year and a half ago, and in a harangue an hour long, assailed that address and the College Board, will compare the above facts, which are found upon the very first pages of the College records, with the statements he then made, and which he has since repeated, concerning the total failure of Mr. Gale's Plan, and the abandonment of the whole enterprise by the Subscribers *after their first meeting.*

The BOND, required by the Subscribers to be given by the Purchasing Committee for the conveyance of the land held by them to the Trustees of the College, is on file and is as follows:

"Whereas a purchase has been made in Township Eleven north, one East of fourth principal meridian, in Knox county, Illinois, of certain lands as hereinafter described, by Silvanus Ferris of Herkimer county, and Nehemia West of Cayuga county, of the State of New York, *in behalf* of certain persons, Subscribers to a fund for a Western Colony and institutions, on a plan proposed by Rev. G. W. Gale, the title of which is now vested in us, and by the said Subscribers we are instructed to vest this title in their Board of Trust—now therefore we bind ourselves, our heirs and assigns to convey our respective and conjoined interests and titles to the following persons, viz: [Here follow the names of the ten Trustees of the College,] and their associates or successors in office, Trustees of the said Institution, now named Prairie College, in the following property or sections of land, being a part of the above named township 11 north, 1 east of 4th principal meridian, viz: [Description of the land by sections, etc.] so soon as circumstances will admit, and in the mean time *convey* to individual purchasers, by direction of said Trustees; which conveyance shall supersede the conveyance to the said Trust of such portions as have been conveyed to individuals.

In witness whereof we have hereunto set our hands and seals this 8th day of January, 1836.   SILVANUS FERRIS, [L. S.]
NEHEMIAH WEST, [L. S.]"

From the College records, as will soon be shown, it appears that the title to all the land continued to be held by the Purchasing Committee until after a charter had been obtained, in 1837; and that then they conveyed the whole to the corporate Board; and that all persons who in the mean time had purchased any of the land, including Subscribers as well as others, received their deeds from the College.

The note of $10,000, given by Messrs. Gale and Ferris, became due on the last of January, 1836, and was then taken up. Of the money which paid it, $5,300 came from Subscribers; the balance, $4,700 was obtained from the Bank of Ontario, at Utica, on another joint note of Messrs. Gale and Ferris, payable in ninety days. When this note became due, it was paid in part by money received as before, from Subscribers, and in part by a new note for $3,139.78, drawn by the same parties, payable in four months. This note was due on the first day of September, 1836, at which time enough money had been received from the Subscribers to pay the largest part of it. The balance, amounting to $1,200, was put into a new note, payable in four months. This last note, after two partial payments, and two renewals for the balance, was entirely paid in March, 1837, by Mr. Ferris, with his own money. These facts are set forth in the books of the Treasurer of the College, and in a letter written by Mr. Ferris a few days after the last payment had been made.

It is no more than simple justice at this point to remark that all the records and facts relating to the founding of the College show that while great credit is due to all the Subscribers for what was accomplished, yet much the largest share of this credit is due to Mr. Gale and Mr. Silvanus Ferris. Without their efforts Knox College would, doubtless, never have been founded. Mr. Gale originated the plan, secured the Subscribers, and risked all that he possessed in order to insure success. Mr. Ferris was a wealthy farmer, and it was his responsible name, joined with Mr. Gale's, which secured the largest part of the money required to purchase the lands for the College. It was his credit, also, that continued that loan until those of the Subscribers who had not yet paid their subscription, could do so without inconvenience to themselves. After all this, he then abandoned a pleasant home in central New York, where he had gathered around him everything that seems desirable in the declining period of life, and at the advanced age of sixty-four years, removed, among the first colonists, to Galesburg, there to share in the privations and cares incident to all pioneer life. This he did wholly for the sake of the College. Happily his life has been spared and the clearness and vigor of his mind, until now, at almost *four*-score years and ten, he sees Knox College richly endowed, having large and costly buildings, and promising to accomplish in the future a nobler mission than even its prayerful and hopeful founders dared anticipate for it.

It is a fortunate thing that no uncertainty rests upon the question, who were these Subscribers who founded the College. The original subscription-book used by Mr. Gale, is in the hands of the Secretary of the College, and contains the names of all the Subscribers. On the first pages of this book are the printed circular and plan of Mr. Gale, immediately following which is this heading: "We, the Subscribers, agree to pay the sums set opposite to our names respectively, to such person or persons as shall be designated by the Subscribers, or Board of Trustees elected by them, for the purposes, and in the manner set forth in the foregoing printed *Preamble and Plan* for establishing literary institutions in the West." This is followed by the names of forty-six persons, as Subscribers. Some of these persons had withdrawn from the enterprise before the first meeting of the Subscribers. It will be remembered that the agent, in his report, after stating that the number on his list was forty-six, added that "there were a few who subscribed, but who, discouraged about our making a purchase, have settled in Michigan." These and some others, making twelve in all, never met with the Subscribers, and never shared either in their counsels or in their pecuniary obligations. They never were regarded by the other Subscribers, from the time of their first meeting onward, as in any manner connected with them in their Association. The remaining thirty-four names alone designate the persons referred to in the foregoing documents as the "Subscribers," by whom the College was founded. Their names are found, not only in the subscription book, but also in the

"Memorandum of Sales," and in the "Treasurer's Books," which are referred to in the minutes of the third meeting, in connection with the distribution of the lands. These last named documents show necessarily who were the true "Subscribers," for they contain the names of the persons who at that third meeting received farm-lands for their subscription, according to the original plan. The Records of the College also contain many of their names. The Records, the "Treasurer's Books" and the "Memorandum of Sales" give thirty-four of the names that are contained in the subscription book, and they give no others, as the Subscribers. The College Board opened its treasury books, consisting of a "Blotter," a "Journal," and a "Ledger," with the names of those Subscribers. Fortunately, also, several of the principal men among them, Mr. Gale, Mr. Ferris and Professor Losey, are now living in Galesburg. These men were familiar with the names of their associates, and they all affirm the correctness of the list contained in the foregoing documents. The account books of the College were opened and were kept for years afterward by Professor Losey, as Treasurer of the College, and the names of the original Subscribers were entered by him in those books.

The names of these Subscribers are given below, together with the amount which each one pledged in return for farm-lands at their meeting, in January, 1836. The sum of these pledges, as will be seen, exceeded by several thousand dollars the whole cost of the land and all the expenses attending its purchase. In other words, these men not only paid for all the land which they donated to the College, but they also put several thousand dollars of money into its treasury. The church relations of the Subscribers, at the time they founded the College, are given in this connection also; but the abundant and positive testimony upon which the statement is based, which of necessity is of some length, will not be given until after some other matters have first been introduced. The Subscribers were all church members except Mr. Thomas Gilbert, one of the Exploring Committee. He was at that time, and has always been since, a Presbyterian in sentiment, and a supporter of a Presbyterian church, of which his wife has, during the whole period, been a member. Mr. Timothy B. Jervis, at the time he served as one of the Exploring Committee, was a candidate for the ministry, and very soon after was licensed and ordained a Presbyterian minister, by his Presbytery in New York.

FOUNDERS OF KNOX COLLEGE.

PRESBYTERIAN MINISTERS:

NAME.	RESIDENCE.	AMOUNT OF PURCHASE.
1. Rev. Geo. W. Gale,	Whitesboro', N. Y.	$3,980
2. " Hiram H. Kellogg,	Clinton, "	2,400
3. " John Waters,	New Hartford, "	2,480
4. " Timothy B. Jervis,	Rome, "	400
5. " Phineas Camp,	Norway, "	560
6. " John Gray,	Troy, "	320
7. " John Frost,	Whitesboro', "	640

Total by Presbyterian Ministers..................$10,780

PRESBYTERIAN ELDERS:

8. Nehemiah West,	Ira, N. Y.	$1,480
9. John McMullen,	Western, "	400
10. John C. Smith,	Utica, "	270
11. I. S. Fitch,	Bainbridge, "	400
12. Smith Griffith,	Nassau, "	480
13. Lewis Kinney,	Greenbush, "	400
14. Amatus Robbins,	Troy, "	400
15. Chauncey Peirce,	Troy, "	400
16. Gurdon Grant,	Troy, "	400
17. Samuel Bond,	Adams, "	560

Total by Presbyterian Elders...................$5,190

LAY MEMBERS OF PRESBYTERIAN CHURCHES:

18. Silvanus Ferris,	Russia, N. Y.	$3,160
19. Nehemiah H. Losey,	Whitesboro', "	600
20. Sylvester Bliss,	Adams, "	960
21. Roland Sears,	Whitesboro', "	400
22. Silvanus Town,	Troy, "	480
23. H. Troop Avery, } 24. George Avery, }	New Lebanon, "	1,600
25. James Barton,	Schoharie, "	800
26. Sidney Rice,	Troy, "	400
27. Miss Araminta P. Rice,	Troy, "	320
28. J. B. Marsh,	Amsterdam, "	400
29. Thos. Gilbert, (see above),	Rome, "	480

Total by Presbyterian Church Members.........$9,600

CONGREGATIONALIST:

30. Thomas Simmons,	Hamilton, N. Y.	$800

By Presbyterians......................$25,570
By Congregationalists.................... 800

Total...............................$26,370

ITS FOUNDERS.   29

To the foregoing list must be added the names of four persons who were Subscribers, and who aided by their counsels and labors in founding the College, but who purchased no lands, preferring to leave their portion to be sold by the College, when it was found that the other Subscribers had pledged more than enough to pay for all the land bought by the Association. These persons were all Presbyterians:

31. Jeremiah Holt,   Watertown, N. Y., an Elder.
32. George Stedman, Rome,   "
33. Benj. P. Johnson,   "   "
34. Walter Webb,   Adams,   "

The foregoing statement shows, that of the thirty-four Subscribers who founded Knox College, *thirty-three* were Presbyterians, and *one* only was a Congregationalist. It shows, also, that these Subscribers, at their meeting in January, 1836, after having directed their Purchasing Committee to convey all the lands held by them to the College, then bought back for themselves a portion of those lands, at greatly increased prices, pledging to the College treasury, in payment thereof, the sum of twenty-six thousand three hundred and seventy dollars. Of this sum, eight hundred dollars were pledged by a Congregationalist—all the rest was pledged by Presbyterians. The whole sum pledged exceeded the cost of the land, and all expenses of the Association, by about ten thousand dollars. The whole amount of farm lands purchased by the Subscribers at this time was 5,240 acres.

A colony, composed principally of a large number of the Subscribers and their families, removed, as early in 1836 as was possible, upon the ground where the College was to be located. The Institutions of learning, which they had come to build up, soon proved a great attraction to persons who were looking for a new western home for themselves, and early began to draw in settlers from various quarters, and of various shades of religious belief. It soon became evident that the College would have no difficulty in filling its treasury by the sale of its lands—and that the more land it could retain for future sale, the better it would be for its prosperity. Under these circumstances, some of the Subscribers, who had not removed to Galesburg, were induced to allow their lands, which they had bought, to go to the College, instead of the money which they had pledged for them. Eight of them, viz: Messrs. Griffith, Gilbert, Bond, Peirce, Bliss, Marsh, and Rice, and Miss

A. P. Rice, returned in all 720 acres. They did this at a pecuniary sacrifice to themselves, as the land was already worth more than the price at which they had bought it. But their sole object had been to establish the College upon a solid basis, and they cheerfully sacrificed their own interests for its welfare. By their act, the College received a less amount of money from the Subscribers than had been pledged by them at first, but it received, instead thereof, land which was already worth more than the money, and which was continually increasing in value. After the return of these lands, there remained, pledged to be paid by the other Subscribers, nearly twenty-three thousand dollars. The College, however, received from them a larger sum than this, from the fact that during the two years that passed before the Corporate Board began to give any deeds, many of the Subscribers sold a part or the whole of their lands to other settlers, and generally at advanced prices; and in many such instances they allowed the new purchaser to pay the increased amount directly to the College. In one instance Mr. Silvanus Ferris allowed the College to sell for its own benefit four hundred acres of the land taken by him, on the express condition that it should be sold at an advance of one-third upon the price which he was to pay for it. The land taken by Mr. J. Barton was sold very early at an advance of twenty-five per cent. upon the price at which he had taken it, and the College received the money. Several others pursued the same generous course toward the College, so that its treasury received from the Subscribers for their farm lands not less than twenty-five thousand dollars. Less than one-thirtieth of this sum came from a Congregationalist—all the remainder came from Presbyterians. Many of the Subscribers who removed to Galesburg purchased village property, and in this way the College received from them several thousand dollars in addition to the above sum. It has always been the custom of the College to sell its lands upon time when desired, allowing the purchaser usually two or three years within which to pay for them. It often happens that the land thus sold is again sold by the first purchaser, and sometimes it passes in this way through the hands of several parties, before the last payment is made to the College, and before any deed has been given. In such cases the common practice is for the College to give a deed directly to the last purchaser, provided the intermediate parties consent. This practice saves expense, and has its advantages in several ways. But it is evident at once that where such a practice prevails the county records of deeds no longer furnish any correct evidence as to the actual purchaser from the College. They show correctly to whom the deed was given, provided it is on record, but not to whom the College sold its lands, and from whom it received the money paid for them. There are not a few men in Galesburg whose names appear in the recorder's office as purchasers of land from the College, while the fact is they bought of other parties, and paid their money to other parties. The county records never show with certainty who paid the money into the College treasury for its lands—its own treasury books alone show this. Yet, simple as this matter is, it has been strangely overlooked in a recent published report of the Congregational General Association of this State concerning Knox College; and that report very sagely presents a list of names, drawn professedly from the county records, to show who paid money into the College treasury in exchange for its lands. That list, as will be shown in due time, has in it a large apocryphal element; but even if it were entirely correct it would be of no value for the purpose for which it is introduced.

The reader will notice from the foregoing facts, that the Subscribers not only paid the full amount pledged by them in their subscription list, but they paid several thousand dollars more. The statement made of late by Mr. Blanchard and his friends, that only a very small part of the amount subscribed was ever paid, is so far from true, that in fact, as the College books show, *much more than the full amount subscribed was paid by the Subscribers.* Several of them paid two or three-fold more than the sum they had at first subscribed. The reader will bear in mind, also, that when these Subscribers divided among themselves a part of the lands which they had purchased of the government, and pledged the price thereof to the College treasury, they were only carrying out their original plan. By that plan they were to keep a part of the lands for themselves, and were to donate the rest to the College. They found at last that it would be a simpler process to bestow the legal title to the whole upon their newly organized College Board and then take their deeds from that Board, rather than from the Purchasing Committee. In this way they appear as purchasers of lands from the College. But the lands they thus purchased were their own according to the previous plan, and according to a mode of division already agreed upon, when the College was founded. These Subscribers, therefore, while nominally purchasers from the College, were in fact purchasers from themselves, as an Association. For the land appropriated by themselves *they paid enough to cover the cost of all the lands purchased by their Committee, and also to put into the College treasury for its own use about eight thousand dollars.* They also made a free donation of all the land not taken by themselves, to the College, to be sold at such times and to such parties as it pleased.

After the College had been founded, in January, 1836, and had received its donation of lands, several persons, not Subscribers, came forward and became purchasers of farm lands. A few of these persons intended to remove West, and bought for their own benefit—others bought in order to help on the enterprise. They all, except the one first named, retained their lands.

The following are their names:

Rev. L. H. Loss, Presbyterian, New York Mills, N. Y...$	320
" Ira Pettibone, " Whitesboro', N. Y.......	120
R. N. Randall, " " "	1,040
Isaac Mills, " Elder, Columbia, N. Y...	2,020
S. Pomeroy, Presbyterian, (Dr. Hopkins' Church.) Auburn, N. Y................................	800
S. Williams, Presbyterian, Russia, N. Y..............	1,040
Samuel Tompkins, Congregationalist, Hamilton, N. Y...	560
R. Root, (not a church member) Camden, N. Y........	320
Total...$	6,220

Of this amount the sum of $5,900 was actually paid to the College. One Congregationalist paid $560. Presbyterians paid $5,020.

The agent of the College, Rev. Mr. Gale, came to Illinois early in 1836, in order to secure a survey of the town plat, and to provide for the comfort of the colonists. During that year and the next he sold farm lands for the College to a large number of settlers. These persons were almost all strangers to the founders of the College and had known nothing of the enterprise until this time. They came to Galesburg for the sake of advancing their own personal interests, and they bought College lands solely for this purpose. Many of them have been made rich by the lands they then purchased. The College sold to all purchasers upon exactly the same terms. Some of them were Presbyterians, some were Congregationalists, and some belonged to no religious denomination. The authors of the pamphlet already alluded to, entitled "Rights of Congregationalists in Knox College," in order to find some ground on which to rest a claim for the Congregational body, have entirely ignored all the action of the founders of the College; and have presented a list of names of the early settlers in Galesburg, who found the College already established when they came here, and who never donated to it one dollar in money or one acre of land; and have given to these men the credit of having both *founded* and *endowed* the College, and for the reason that *they bought farm lands from the College* — not *for* it, but *from* it — for their own personal benefit! That pamphlet claims, in naked terms, that the men who bought farm lands from the College were, *in so doing*, its founders, and endowers! The folly of such a claim needs no other exposure than its simple statement. The College had already been founded, and all its lands which have endowed it, had been donated to it, before these settlers ever saw or heard of Galesburg. As, however, the question is thus raised, what amount of money has been paid to the College for its farm lands, and by whom, it may be well to present here the facts which will fully answer it. The following list embraces the names of all the purchasers of the original farm lands of the College from the close of the last meeting of the Subscribers in January, 1836, down to the present time. The list will show at a glance who were Congregationalists, and who were Presbyterians, and who belonged to neither party at the time they bought. The total amount of money to be paid by each class of purchasers is also given. This list of names and the sums attached are taken from the treasurer's books, and have been carefully examined by him and found to be correct. The cultivated farm in the original purchase has been sold several times, and as often returned to the College. It is now in the possession of a German, who has not yet paid for it. If paid for, it will not realize enough to cover its cost. For these reasons it is not embraced in the present statement. There are persons not named below who have received deeds from the College, but who purchased either of the Subscribers or of other parties, and paid their money to them or according to their direction. There are others, also, who bought and made one or more partial payments, but who afterward returned the land to the College, and received back the money they had paid. None of these, of course, are named as purchasers. The list here given embraces all who actually bought the original farm lands from the College, and not from the Subscribers or other intermediate parties, and who never returned them. The records of the First Presbyterian Church in Galesburg have furnished the church relations of all but four of those among the purchasers who are classed as Congregationalists or Presbyterians. Two of those four, are W. A. Wood and G. W. G. Ferris, both of whom were members of the Second Presbyterian Church in this city, of which the writer of this was pastor, at the time they bought. They were both decided Presbyterians. The other two are W. B. Hamlin and H. Wilcox, who are classed according to their well-known preferences.

PURCHASERS OF FARM LANDS FROM THE COLLEGE.

PRESBYTERIANS. In 1836–7: B. Allen, E. Pomeroy, E. H. King, Hitchcock Family, H. Conger, A. Tyler, Jr., G. W. Gale, bought eighty acres of the College, W. Holyoke, H. Wilcox, $5,120. In 1854: W. A. Wood, G. W. G. Ferris, $12,480.14.

Total by Presbyterians, $17,600.14.

CONGREGATIONALISTS. In 1836–7: E. Swift, M. Chambers, E. Farnham, L. Sanderson, R. Payne, W. B. Hamlin, $7,920. In 1852: J. Blanchard, $2,400. In 1854: L. Gary, A. B. Clark, $2,840.

Total by Congregationalists, $13,160.

NON-PROFESSORS. In 1836–7: C. S. Colton, M. Miller, L. Chappel, J. Duston, J. West, H. Ferris, $3,320. In 1846: J. Jerauld, $500. In 1850: L. Martin, H. Ferris, $480. In 1852: J. L. Clay, $800. In 1853: A. G. Pearson, $2,400. In 1854: J. H. Barnett, H. C. Foote, $2,569.94. In 1856: J. Thirlwell, W. B. Patterson, $1,500.

Total by Non-Professors, $11,569.94.

OTHER PARTIES. In 1850: W. D. Lee, Baptist. In 1854: S. Richardson, Methodist. Total, $2,000.

Total by all classes, $44,330.08.

In the foregoing list are thirty-seven names. The list of Non-Professors embraces the names of several persons, who, after they had bought of the College, became members of the First Church in this place, while it was purely Presbyterian. Of that number Mr. C. S. Colton, and perhaps one or two others, but not more, are now regarded as Congregationalists. During the first two years after the College had been founded, frequent sales of the farm lands were made. But from the early part of 1838, down to 1850, a period of twelve years, no more farms were sold, except the half of one quarter-section in 1846. It will be seen that the total amount paid by Congregationalists, including Mr. S. Tompkins, who bought in the State of New York, for farm lands, purchased previous to the year 1852, is only $8,480. This is a less sum than that paid by one Presbyterian purchaser, Mr. G. W. G. Ferris, who paid $8,630.14.

It has been shown that the Subscribers paid for the farm lands bought by them, $25,000; and that other parties in the State of New York paid $5,900. These sums added to that paid by all classes named above, give $75,230.08 as the total amount paid into the College treasury for all its original farm lands which have ever been sold. By recalling the statements already made, it will be easy to determine how much of this amount has been paid by Presbyterians and how much by Congregationalists.

PRESBYTERIANS.	CONGREGATIONALISTS.
Subscribers......$24,200	One Subscriber.......$ 800
Others in N. Y.... 5.020	S. Tompkins, in N. Y.. 560
In Galesburg, Ill.. 17,600 14	In Galesburg, Ill..... 13,160
$46,820 14	$14,520

The sum paid by Non-Professors, and by others not included under either of the above heads, is $13,889 94, which is almost equal to the whole sum ever paid by all purchasers who were Congregationalists.

Much has been said of late about the large amount of money paid to the College by the earliest Congregational purchasers; and one of those gentlemen has allowed a statement to be published over his own name, in which he is represented as having done very much to give success to the enterprise during its first years. The following facts will correct the erroneous impressions made by such statements: The only two Congregationalists who bought a large amount of land during the early years of the College, were Mr. Swift and Mr. Chambers. The agent very reluctantly sold to them more land than he had allowed others to take, because they represented themselves as able to control a large amount of capital, which they would secure to the benefit of the colony. Even then, however, the whole sum to be paid by them was, as already shown, only a few thousand dollars. Mr. Chambers was allowed to select, at a merely nominal price, the best business lot in the village, with the clear understanding that he was to erect upon it, at once, a store, and engage in mercantile business. As soon, however, as he had secured the title to his property, he went to the neighboring town of Knoxville, the county seat, and there bought a lot and erected upon it a large store, and for five years employed his capital and energies there, in total indifference to the business interests of Galesburg. He made very little improvement upon his lands, and for many years a large portion of the amount due on them remained unpaid. The College, therefore, was never greatly benefitted by him. The whole sum engaged to be paid by all Congregational purchasers, for farm lands, previous to the year 1852, was only $8,480. Of this, a large portion remained unpaid for many years. Plainly, therefore, the College did not receive very much money from Congregational sources. Mr. Blanchard is represented in the "Rights of Congregationalists" as one of the *early* purchasers of College lands, and as having *paid* for them, greatly to the prosperity of the College. The truth is this: Mr. Blanchard bought his lands for $2,400, in 1852, seventeen years after the College was founded. In 1857, when he was removed from the Presidency, he had *paid the interest* on the amount and no more. The College then *donated* him $1,400, and credited him with that sum on his note. After this was done, he brought in a bill of $200 against the College, which was allowed, and then modestly asked for the balance of his note. His request was not granted, and the note remains unpaid. In this way he assisted in "starting" the College, with his money. These trifles would not have been noticed, had not the "Rights of Congregationalists" claimed that Knox College owes nearly all its success to the money paid for its farm lands by Congregationalists, and that it was especially their money "which started the College," and which has endowed it. The simple truth concerning all of them is, that practically *the College has endowed them.* Galesburg owes its intelligence, and enterprise, and consequent prosperity to the College.

PRAIRIE COLLEGE.

The Board of Trustees, appointed by the founders of the College, met on the 8th day of January, 1836, the day after their appointment, in Whitesboro', New York, and organized, and transacted some business, of which the following items are of present interest: " Voted that Gale and Ferris be a committee to provide for building a College edifice and house of entertainment:" " Voted that Messrs. Gale and West be a committee to provide for a mill, and for cultivating College lands :" " Voted that H. H. Kellogg be a committee to devise plans, etc , for a Female Seminary." The Board met again, in the same place, on the 2nd day of March, following, when it was "Voted that a boarding-house, of one and a half stories high, twenty-six by thirty-six feet on the ground, be immediately erected:" "Voted that N. H. Losey be appointed a surveyor for the colony, and that the expense of surveying be paid out of the College fund." The reader will bear in mind that these two meetings of the Board were held in New York, before a single settler had found his way to Galesburg, and before an acre of land had been sold there. At these meetings it was determined to proceed immediately to erect a College edifice, a house of entertainment, a mill, a boarding-house, and to prepare plans for a Female Seminary. These facts show clearly that the founders of the College had already provided the means which would "*start it;*" and that they did not depend alone upon future sales of land for the first movement.

The Board met again at New Hartford, N. Y., August 31st, 1836, when it was "Resolved that a Committee of five be appointed to inquire into the propriety of applying to the Legislature for an act of incorporation, the ensuing winter, and to make such application if by them it be deemed expedient."

A petition for a charter was prepared, in which the names of eleven persons were designated as Trustees; the Board when full was to consist of twenty-five members, including the President of the College; the remainder of the Board were to be appointed by those already designated. The petition was acted upon, and a charter granted by the Legislature of Illinois, in February, 1837, at Vandalia. In the Charter the name was changed from "Prairie College" to "Knox Manual Labor College." (The name was changed to "KNOX COLLEGE" by act of Legislature, in February, 1857; the "Manual Labor" system having been abandoned at an early date.) The new Board appointed in the Charter, did not meet and organize until in August, 1837. In the mean time, the Board of Prairie College continued to act, as it did also for some months after the new organization. Under date of March 28th, 1837, at Galesburg, they "Resolved that a Committee of three be appointed to fix on a spot for a permanent burying ground for the colony, to lay out and procure a survey of the same," etc. At the same meeting, the "Committee on Rents reported that there were six houses belonging to the Trustees, besides the school house." It was also "Voted that a Committee of three be appointed to inquire into the condition of the funds, lands, etc., belonging to the Trustees, and everything pertaining to the College, that this Board may be prepared to make a correct statement to the new Board, and to convey to them the property of this Board."

"April 20th, 1837: Voted that five acres, or the south half of the ten acre lot, on the west side of the village plat, and extending north to Main street, be laid out for a burying ground:" also "Voted that the College buildings be erected directly south of Broad street, sixty rods from the street running east and west on the south side of the village."

"June 15th, 1837: Voted that the treasurer be instructed to loan to Mr. John Kendall two thousand dollars:" also "Voted to loan the Mill Company a sum not to exceed $1,500."

"July 21st, 1837: Voted that the Chairman call the incorporated Board of Trustees of Knox Manual Labor College to meet on the second Wednesday of August, at the house of John G. Sanborn of Knoxville:" also "Voted that all the College lands on sections fourteen and twenty-three, making three hundred and twenty acres, be deeded to persons in trust, for the purpose of a Theological Seminary." At a subsequent meeting, on the 1st day of August, 1837, the same Board voted "that the south-east block of the village plat, as it now is, be reserved for the *site* of a Theological Seminary, if it should be wanted for that purpose." These lands, thus set apart for a Theological Seminary, were designed exclusively for a Presbyterian Seminary. This was the intention of the donors, as they have always claimed, and the committee who held the land in trust always acted in view of that intention, and always held the land for the Presbyterian body, and for no other. When it was proposed, a few years ago, to establish a New School Presbyterian Theological Seminary in the North-west, this property was offered as an inducement to locate the institution in Galesburg. The Seminary was not located there, and in 1853 the land all reverted to the College. The three hundred and twenty acres had been included, in the mean time, within the corporate limits of the city, and nearly all have since been sold at high prices. A large share of the present funds of the College has been derived from the sale of these lands. *The town property has ever been the chief source of wealth to the College.* This property has been bought by all classes of people, having all shades of religious belief. If the control of the College were to be vested, in accordance with the latest claim, in those who have paid their money into its treasury in exchange for its lands, the College Board would embrace the representatives of almost all forms of belief that are known "under the whole heavens." And the share of Congregationalists in such a Board, for their portion of money paid, would be small indeed.

"NEW ORGANIZATION."

"*August* 9th, 1837 : Trustees of Knox Manual Labor College met for the first time, at the house of Matthew Chambers, of Knoxville. Present—John Waters, George W. Gale, John G. Sanborn, George H. Wright, Parnach Owen, Erastus Swift, Thomas Simmons, Matthew Chambers, Nehemiah West and N. H. Losey.

John Waters was chosen President, N. H. Losey, Clerk, and John G. Sanborn, Treasurer, for the term of one year.

On motion, it was resolved that Wm. Holyoke, Peter Butler, of Monmouth, and Silvanus Ferris be added to the Board of Trustees.

On motion, the following preamble and resolution were adopted :

WHEREAS, an Association of gentlemen, in the State of New York, was formed with a view of establishing a College, and other Seminaries, in this State, and *having purchased lands and raised funds for said object*, in Knox county, township eleven north, of range one east, of the fourth principal meridian ; and whereas, by a petition from said Association and others, a charter for a College and Preparatory School, with power to add Professorships of Law and Medicine, in said township, has been granted by the Legislature of this State ; we, the persons named as Trustees in said charter, have been organized this day: And whereas, the said Association have proposed to make over said property to this Board,

Resolved, That we will receive said property, and all of it, with the express design of carrying into effect *the original purpose* of said Association, so far as the charter and the means in our hands, or to be received, shall permit.

On motion, *Resolved*, That a committee of three be appointed for six months, to execute the orders of the Board of Trustees.

Resolved, That the committee above named, who shall be styled the Executive Committee, be authorized to sell and dispose of the lands which may be granted to this Board, under such regulations as have been heretofore adopted by the Association, denominated the ' Trustees of Prairie College,' and that said Executive Committee be governed by the resolutions and orders of said Association in the management of the property and funds belonging to, or which may be deeded to this Board."

The Corporate Board having fully organized, the former Board met "January 19th, 1838," when " on motion, it was *Resolved*, That deeds of all the Colony purchase be made from the Purchasing Committee to the Corporate Board of Trustees, and from them to individuals ; except such parts of the purchase as were laid out into village property, and such other property as is designed for the benefit of a Theological Seminary."

"*Resolved*, That the above excepted property be deeded directly from the Purchasing Committee to a Committee of Trust, who shall manage it according to the instructions to be contained in the deed of conveyance."

The same Board, at a meeting held " Feb. 12th, 1838, *Resolved*,

That it is expedient to deed the village property to the incorporated Board of Trustees; and that the property designed for the benefit of a Theological Seminary only be deeded to a Committee of Trust."

"Feb. 19th, 1838. *Resolved*, That the south-east quarter of block 24, be reserved for a meeting house."

"A meeting of the Trustees of Knox Manual Labor College was held March 7th, 1838," at which, after enumerating the donations of lots made by the old Board for a burying ground, a meeting-house, etc., it was "*Resolved*, That said burying ground be deeded to the Trustees of THE PRESBYTERIAN SOCIETY OF GALESBURG; and that the meeting-house and parsonage lots be deeded also *to said trustees*, for the uses mentioned above."

"*Resolved*, That the President and Secretary be directed to give deeds *to all who have purchased land of the former proprietors*, on the conditions of the purchase as specified in their books: Provided, the purchasers give sufficient security to this Board for moneys unpaid on such purchase."

"*Resolved*, That all deeds for lands in this township, given by this Board, have a clause attached to the same prohibiting the manufacture or sale of intoxicating drinks."

The last resolution was soon after modified so as to apply only to village property, and not to farms.

The foregoing records and other facts taken from the College books, show conclusively that the act of the Subscribers at their last meeting in founding the College, was not a mere form, but that the College was in the fullest sense founded at that time. They show that the Subscribers at that meeting not only founded the College, but also endowed it—how abundantly we shall soon see. They show that from the beginning the College had money in its treasury, and that very little of that money came from Congregationalists. The College funds in 1836, the first year of its existence, were in such a state that the Board were able to expend in purchasing timber and new prairie lands and other property, a sum exceeding $9,000. The treasurer stated in a report dated May 1st, 1838, a few weeks only after the date of the last record given above, that the "available funds" of the College and the interest due thereon, amounted to $24,158.58. By "available funds" in these reports is meant the notes and other securities held by the College, upon which it received interest: The phrase includes no other kinds of property. The next year, "Nov. 5, 1839," the "available funds" were reported to amount to $29,714.86, *after paying all the indebtedness of the Board*. In 1843, when the Academy and Preparatory Department had been in complete operation five years, and the College two years, and when heavy expenses had been incurred for buildings and other improvements, the "available funds," which remained unexhausted, were reported as amounting to $26,068.56. The total value, at that time, of all the College property, was stated in the same report to be equal to $74,514.56. From that time until the present, the farm lands and village property of the College have continually advanced in value, and although large sums of money have been expended for instruction and for buildings and other objects, yet the "available funds" have steadily increased until now they amount to near $206,000. The total value of all the property owned by the College at the present time, is about $400,000.

THE ENDOWMENT.

The following facts will show the sources from which the endowment of the College has been derived, and also the total value of all the property which it has ever owned:

1. The principal source of all the wealth of the College has been the lands donated by its founders. Of SIX HUNDRED THOUSAND DOLLARS' worth of property, which the College has held, as will soon be shown, all but about *forty-six thousand dollars*' worth, has been derived from those lands. The founders also donated eight thousand dollars in money—this sum being the excess which they paid into the College treasury above the entire cost of the whole enterprise down to the time the donation was made. The public will judge whether the men who made those donations of land and money to a College of their own creating are not entitled to the credit of having endowed it.

2. The Rev. H. H. Kellogg, while President of the College, obtained, when in England, in 1844, at the World's Convention, a small donation, in money and in books, valued at about $2,000.

In 1844, Rev. G. W. Gale obtained among his personal friends in New York and elsewhere about 1,600 volumes of books for the College library, and over $2,000 in money, a part of which was expended for a philosophical apparatus. He also obtained some other articles, which were sold for the College. Mr. Gale states that the greater part of these donations came from gentlemen connected with Presbyterian, Episcopalian and Unitarian churches. In New England he obtained some money, chiefly from gentlemen in Boston, among whom were Messrs. Lawrence, Appleton, Lowell, Peter Brooks, and their friends, none of whom were Congregationalists. These donations were about equal to $4,000.

3. In 1844, J. P. Williston, Esq., a Congregationalist, of North Hampton, Mass., became interested in the College, through Mr. Gale, its agent at the time, and commenced making small donations, of a few hundred dollars each year, which he continued for a period of eleven years. At the end of the eleven years, when his donations ceased, he had contributed to the College funds, according to the treasurer's books, about $8,000. Mr. Blanchard has credited him with $2,000 more than this amount, but that sum was given principally to indigent students, and not to the College. Mr. Williston had been a donor to the College two years before Mr. Blanchard became its President. After that event, his donations were devoted almost wholly to the salary of Mr. Blanchard. In a letter written by him two years ago, since Mr. Blanchard's removal from the College, and published at the time in Galesburg, he distinctly declared that in contributing to Knox College, he had no interest in the question whether it was to be under Presbyterian or Congregational control.

The reader will bear in mind that when Mr. Williston commenced his small annual donations, the College property was worth about $80,000, of which amount, nearly $30,000 were "available funds." At the end of eleven years, his donations ceased, because the College was then too rich to need what he could give. It is simply absurd, therefore, to claim, as the "Rights of Congregationalists" does, that "in a dark and trying hour, he came forward" and saved the College; and that the donations made at that period, principally by him, were so valuable, that without them "*all the previous endowments and property*" would have been entirely consumed in current expenses, and the very life of the institution endangered." Mr. Williston is a man of honorable sentiments, and would not willingly suffer his friends to magnify unduly and to the injury of others, the importance of his benefactions. His donations were made from generous impulses, and his name will ever be cherished by the College, as one of its benefactors. But the College did not depend upon him for its life.

4. The Society for promoting Collegiate and Theological education at the West, began to aid Knox College in 1846, and continued its aid until 1855, when the College had become so prosperous as to need no further aid from that source. Rev. Theron Baldwin,

Corresponding Secretary of that Society, in a letter addressed to the writer, gives "the sum of $5,864.88, as standing on the books of the Society, charged to Knox College."

5. In 1853, the Hon. Charles Phelps, of Cincinnati, Ohio, donated to the College, eighteen quarter-sections of land, lying in Illinois. The donation was made, not to the general funds of the College, but for the specific purpose of establishing and supporting one or more new professorships. The lands were not to be sold until they would bring ten dollars an acre, or a total of $28,880. The following statement, made by John G. Sanborn, Esq., of Knoxville, a member of the Board of Trustees of the College, and agent of Mr. Phelps for many years, will show the value of the land when the donation was made.

"I was, for several years, agent for Charles Phelps, Esq., late of Cincinnati, Ohio, and had a full list of the lands which he owned in Illinois, and was familiar with the value of them, and regularly paid the taxes for him, and at the time of his donation to Knox College I estimated the value of the lands donated by him, to be from *twelve to fifteen thousand dollars.*

JOHN G. SANBORN.

KNOXVILLE, July 5, 1859.

In the report of the Treasurer presented to the Board at its annual meeting in June, 1854, one year after the donation had been received, it was reported as worth $20,356.95. Since that time, all the land, but four quarter-sections, has been sold. The title to three of these quarter-sections is disputed, and is, perhaps, worthless. The last report of the Treasurer, presented in June, 1859, states that the amount received for the portion of these lands sold, is ($24,672.15) twenty-four thousand six hundred and seventy-two dollars and fifteen cents. The same report estimates the four quarter-sections unsold as worth $10 an acre, which would make their entire value equal to $6,400. The College has an undisputed right to only one of them, the value of which is $1,600. This sum, added to the above, gives the entire present value of this donation at $26,272.15. After these statements by the agent of Mr. Phelps and by the Treasurer of the College, the reader is asked to notice the statement concerning the same matter made in the " Rights of Congregationalists," which, it will be remembered, is a report presented at the last annual meeting of the Congregational General Association of this State, and adopted, *as true,* by the unanimous vote of that body, as their own minutes declare. That report, after stating truly, but indefinitely, that the present endowment of Knox College is " from three to four hundred-thousand dollars in amount," then adds as follows: "The present endowment of the College *is almost entirely* THE PROCEEDS of the gift of Hon. Charles Phelps, a Congregationalist." And again it says: "We are next called to consider the munificent gift of the late Hon. Charles Phelps, who gave to the College eighteen quarter-sections of land, in Illinois, estimated to be worth *at the time* $30,000, and *now* constituting *the principal part* of the College endowment of over $300,000." The same report represents the donation as having been made to the College at a time when, without this "timely aid," the College must have exhausted all its other property in mere "current expenses," and have become entirely bankrupt—(p. 26.) If the committee who drew up that report, and if the Association who adopted it, knew anything of the matter, they must have known that Mr. Phelps' donation was not made to the College until in 1853, after it had become comparatively rich; they must have known, also, that the College has received from that donation less than $25,000 in money; they must have known, also, that, even had the "*proceeds*" been large, and had the College at the same time been poor and embarrassed, yet these funds of Mr. Phelps could, in no manner, have relieved the College and have saved its other property, for those funds were given for the specific purpose of endowing new professorships, and could be used for no other purpose; they must have known that *their entire statement was false.* But if they knew nothing of the matter, with certainty, then why publish such statements as "indubitable facts?" The chairman of the committee by whom the above report was drawn up has, since its publication, announced in the "Congregational Herald," that their "statement that the present funds of the College were *chiefly* derived from the gift of land by Judge Phelps is *not correct.*" Yet he says "the error in *no wise affects* the position of the report; *it does not vary in any case the general result!*" Think of that, dear reader, an error of over $300,000 is such a mere trifle that " it in *no wise* effects the position of the report!" Is not that a sublime self-confidence! The report is to be taken as strictly accurate in every other respect, notwithstanding the admission of so grave an error in respect to a matter wherein it was so easy to know and state the exact truth. The admission of so serious a mistake in respect to so simple a matter *does* very materially "affect the position of the report;" *it at once destroys all confidence in the whole report.* If the committee did not know the truth about this matter, how shall we believe that they knew it about other matters ?

The denominational relations of Judge Phelps, when his donation was made, will appear from the following statements, made with direct reference to this point, by Rev. Samuel W. Fisher, D. D., President of Hamilton College, New York, but for many years previous to last year, pastor of the Second Presbyterian Church in Cincinnati.

"HAMILTON COLLEGE, CLINTON, Dec. 9, 1858.

"Judge Phelps came to Cincinnati from Vermont, some little time before I came to that city, *more than twelve years ago.* In Vermont he was connected with a Congregational Church. He began to attend my church *soon after* I took charge of it. He *purchased* a pew in it, *and attended there until the day of his death.* I attended his funeral. His widow occupies the same pew, and is still an attendant there. A daughter and a son-in-law, now residing with their mother, united with my church on profession last July, just before my leaving. Judge Phelps was an attendant there when he made the donation to Knox College. I do not think Judge Phelps, if alive, would be much concerned as to which denomination had the control of the College. His mind did not occupy itself with the points that distinguish them. His object was to promote Christian education at the West. Most certainly *he had not*, nor has his widow, or any of his children with whom I have an acquaintance, any objection to having the College under Presbyterian control. As members of a Presbyterian Church, several of them would naturally prefer it.

SAMUEL W. FISHER."

From the above explicit testimony of Dr. Fisher, it is evident that, unless it be wholly impossible to fall from the grace of Congregationalism after having once so much as *professed* it, Judge Phelps had totally abandoned his connection with that system during at least the last twelve years of his life. This will appear the more certain from the well known fact that, *before* he left Vermont *he had left the Congregational Church* there, from some dissatisfaction, and had attended the Baptist Church. He had been some seven years a constant attendant upon and a supporter of a Presbyterian Church in Cincinnati *when he made his donation* to Knox College. In justice to himself and to his surviving family, therefore, his donation is to be credited to the Presbyterian body, and not to the Congregational. The reader will no doubt be interested in knowing how this matter concerning Judge Phelps is stated in the "Rights of Congregationalists." That report says: "Mr.

Phelps was *in sentiment* a Congregationalist, though *not* a church member. By reason of a local difficulty, he left and went to the Baptist Church, with which his wife subsequently united, and *in that denomination* he continued to worship at the East, and after his removal to the West, *during the remainder of his life.*" Compare that statement with President Fisher's declaration, that during the last twelve years of his life, Judge Phelps attended the Presbyterian Church, of which he, Dr. Fisher, was pastor.

The *logic* of the report is not less remarkable than its *facts*. Its argument is this: first, that Mr. Phelps was never a member of any Congregational Church—then, that while in Vermont, he gave up all attendance upon even the religious services of that body, and became an attendant upon those of a Baptist Church, with which his wife united as a member—and then, that after removing to the West, and " during the remainder of his life," he had no further connection with the Congregational Church, but remained with the Baptist— and *therefore* "he was a Congregationalist!"

The entire amount of property ever owned by the College, has come from the sources above enumerated, except a few hundred dollars derived from uncertain sources. It will be seen that no account is made of money received for tuition in the various departments of the institution. There were ninety-four and a half scholarships attached to the first lands sold, each scholarship entitling the holder to send a pupil for instruction for the period of twenty-five years, to either the Academy, the Preparatory Department, the Young Ladies' Seminary, or the College. These scholarships, when not used by the owners, have commonly been sold to students from year to year, at a rate a little less than the price of tuition in the several departments of the College. Hence very little money has ever been received from students. The Academy, from which nearly all the money paid for tuition is received, has been for several years an expense to the College Board, although it has had from two hundred to three hundred students each year.

The Academy and the Preparatory Department of the College, were opened in 1838. The first class entered the College in 1841. A "Female Collegiate Department," which is a fully organized Seminary for young ladies, having its own separate corps of instructors, and its own buildings, has been in successful operation for several years. All these departments are under the control of the College Board, and all alike depend upon the same general funds for their support. For the management of its property—for insurance—for taxes, which until recently had to be paid—for loss on buildings destroyed by fire, and by wear of time—for agents—for teachers—for lands donated to churches and railroad companies—for village lots thrown open to the public as a park, and not included in the lands reported by the treasurer, as a part of present property—for all such expenses, the College has paid out, lost or donated, as estimated by the treasurer—by the former agents—and by several trustees, an amount considerably more than $200,000. That this estimate is very much too small, can be seen from the fact that during the last *four* years alone, the cost of instruction and the care of buildings, excluding all other expenses, has been about $60,000.

The last annual report of the Treasurer states the present value of the College property, including money, lands and buildings, at $366,095.15. This sum includes $26,272.15, the present value of the Phelps Fund, which amount, if deducted from the former, will leave $339,823.

The reader is now in possession of all the facts relating to the money and lands ever donated to the College. That the whole matter may be taken in at a single view, the several facts above given are here presented in a brief

RECAPITULATION.

Donated by Subscribers *in money*..........	$8,000 00
" through Messrs. Kellogg and Gale..	6,000 00
" by J. P. Williston................	8,000 00
" by College Society...............	5,864 88
" by Charles Phelps, present value...	26,272 15
Other College property, at present time......	339,823 00
Am't expended, donated, lost etc., from 1836,	200,000 00
Total............................	$593,960 03

It thus appears that the entire value of all the property ever owned by the College is almost *six hundred thousand dollars*. The several donations made by *all parties* who were not Subscribers, it will be seen, amount to $46,137.03. This sum deducted from the total amount ever owned by the College, leaves $547,823. And this sum of FIVE HUNDRED AND FORTY-SEVEN THOUSAND, EIGHT HUNDRED AND TWENTY-THREE DOLLARS, *is the product of that donation of land and money made to the College by the men who founded it.* All the other donations, except that made by Mr. Phelps, which has only become available within the last three or four years, were exhausted immediately in current expenses. The endowment of the College has come wholly from the donation made by the Subscribers and by Mr. Phelps. Let the statement be repeated here, that of almost six hundred thousand dollars, all but about forty-six thousand came from the donation made by the founders of the College. The men who gave that property were all Presbyterians but one, who was a Congregationalist. The money paid by that one, was less than one-thirtieth of the whole amount paid by the Subscribers, in order to found and endow the College. One-thirtieth of the entire proceeds of the original donation, $547,823, amounts to $18,260.77, which is to be credited to Congregationalists; while the balance, amounting to $529,562.23, is to be credited to Presbyterians.

By crediting each denomination with the amount of all the donations made by parties connected with it, we shall be able to see how much has been given by Congregationalists and how much by Presbyterians.

CONGREGATIONAL DONATIONS.

By one Subscriber, proceeds of lands	$18,260 77
" J. P. Williston	8,000 00
" College Society, one half	2,932 44
Total by Congregationalists	$29,193 21

PRESBYTERIAN DONATIONS.

By Subscribers	$529,562 23
" Messrs. Kellogg and Gale, as above	6,000 00
" College Society, one half	2,932 44
" Charles Phelps	26,272 15
Total by Presbyterians	$564,766 82

Thus it is seen the College has received from Congregational sources, from the time it was founded, until now, property equal in value to twenty-nine thousand, one hundred and ninety-three dollars and twenty-one cents. During the same time, it has received from Presbyterian sources, property equal to five hundred and sixty-four thousand, seven hundred and sixty-six dollars and eighty-two cents. These facts will show the "Rights of Congregationalists in Knox College." Yet the reader must remember the whole Plan originated with Presbyterians. It was their wisdom and their energy, that secured the success of that Plan. They originated that Plan with no purpose or thought of inviting other denominations to become partners with them in it. They *did* intend to build up a College for the wants of the West, and not of a denomination, but they did *not* intend to put the control of that College into any other hands than Presbyterians. They called no convention of different denominations to consult about the work, and to take part with them in its accomplishment. There was no recognized *union* of denominations in founding Knox College. It was a private enterprise, by members of the Presbyterian Church. One Congregationalist joined with them for his own personal benefit; but his connection did not vary the character of the Plan in any degree. He made no stipulations for himself as a Congregationalist. Had he proposed any they would have been peremptorily rejected. The Plan was developed,—the work was in progress when he united in it. He did his part worthily among the founders of the College, and he shall ever receive his full share of the credit which belongs to those founders. But in the inception and shaping of that Plan, he had no part. When received as a Subscriber, it was with no condition, express or implied, that through him was to be transmitted to the whole Congregational body, for all time to come, a perfect right of inheritance and control in the College. Such a right he never claimed; such a right never was granted. Indeed, it probably was not known to more than one of the other Subscribers, that Mr. Simmons was a Congregationalist when the College was founded. This appears from the testimony of the founders given below. While it is true that as a question of *right*, the Congregationalists had no partnership in the College, or at most, only a share equal to one-thirtieth of the whole, it is nevertheless true that the College *has been, and ever will be conducted on most liberal principles toward them.* They have always been generously represented in the Board and in the Faculty. They have more members now among the Trustees, than Presbyterians have; and they constitute a majority of the College Faculty. The Presbyterian members of the Board have voted unanimously for every Congregationalist in the Faculty. They have unanimously elected Congregationalists as Trustees. They *did not* elect as many of that denomination as are now found in the Board. Some of those who were selected from the Ministry and Eldership of the Presbyterian Church, and were appointed to the Board because they were Presbyterians, as they professed, have since become the most decided Congregationalists. In this way has the present strength of Congregationalists in the College Board been secured.

TESTIMONY OF THE FOUNDERS.

In determining the denominational relations of the founders of the College, and the question to whom its control, both legally and morally belongs, the public can have nothing more reliable than the testimony of those founders themselves. The founders of a College have a right, both in law and equity, to determine into whose hands it shall be placed. They are the most competent witnesses to settle a controversy as to what their own intentions were. They know with certainty to what body of Christians, if to any, they belonged; and hence their statements on the point must settle the question. A large collection of letters and certificates has been received from the founders of Knox College, respecting these questions. The testimony is uniform and unhesitating, that they were, with but one exception, Presbyterians; and most of them did not know of even that one exception. They declare explicitly, that they had no thought of transmitting the control of the College to any others than Presbyterians. The recent attempt to make it appear that these men, even if nominally Presbyterians, were so only by connection with "Plan-of-Union" Churches, and were in fact Congregationalists, will be set at rest by the men themselves. Moreover, as the list of the founders will show, a large number of them were Elders of churches, and every one who knows what a "Plan-of-Union" Church is, knows that one of its essential features is that it has no Elders.

Mr. Blanchard, who always counts largely upon either the ignorance or the credulity of the public, in his statements, has ventured so far as to speak, in a printed letter of his, two years ago, of a "Plan-of-Union Presbyterian, *a ruling Elder.*" No man knew better than he that "Plan-of-Union" Churches had no "ruling Elders;" and he knew also, that the man of whom he spoke, Mr. N. West, was a "ruling Elder" in that church which he called "Plan-of-Union," and was moreover a decided Presbyterian.

In addition to the Elders, the list of founders shows a large number of Presbyterian ministers, and these will hardly be claimed as Congregationalists, even by those who are able to believe in "Plan-of-Union ruling Elders." It is worthy of remark in this connection, that the "Rights of Congregationalists" uniformly assumes that a member of a Plan-of-Union Church is *ipso facto, not* a Presbyterian, and *is* a Congregationalist.

The first letter given below, from the founders of the College, is very properly that of Rev. George W. Gale, D. D., who originated the Plan, and whose efforts were the principal means of carrying it into successful operation.

LETTER OF REV. G. W. GALE, D. D.

"I was born in the State of New York, and graduated at Union College. I studied for the Ministry in Princeton Theological Seminary, was licensed to preach by the Presbytery of Hudson, and was ordained by the Presbytery of St. Lawrence, now Watertown. While I have always cherished feelings of great kindness and brotherly love toward Christians of other denominations, and have rejoiced in whatever contributed to their true prosperity, yet in all my preferences, and in all my professions, I have always been a Presbyterian. While I have admired many things in the history of Congregationalism, yet my clearest convictions have ever been, that the apostolic church was not modelled after that fashion.

The Plan for founding Knox College originated with me. I spent much time and money in maturing the Plan and in enlisting my friends in it. The great object of my life, since the College has been founded, has been to make it an institution second to no other in its means of furnishing a thorough education to its students, and one which should be worthy of the most liberal patronage of the public. It was never my design to found a sectarian College. It was to be a College open to all the youth of our land, without any reference to their relations to Christian denominations. But while the College was founded *for* all denominations, it was not founded *by* all. *It was exclusively a Presbyterian enterprise. It was always so understood among all its founders.* The Subscribers to my Plan, by whom the College was founded, were all secured by myself, and I was well acquainted with their Church relations. They were all decided Presbyterians except Mr. Simmons, who was a Congregationalist. A large number of them were ministers and elders in the Presbyterian Church, and almost all were my personal friends. Mr. Simmons heard of our Plan and became a Subscriber, but with no purpose, on that account, of claiming any share in the control of the College as a Congregationalist. We never expected to yield the College to any others than those who should represent our own opinions as Presbyterians. If others were invited to share in that control, it was only as a matter of comity, and for the sake of the prosperity of the College, and not from any original right which they had. The intention of the founders in respect to the future control of the College is clearly evinced by their action in appointing the Board of " Prairie College," and afterward in appointing the corporate Board. The men to whom they committed their College in both Boards were almost all Presbyterians. As the coöperation of others was desirable, they elected, during the early years of the College, some from among the Episcopal, the Congregational, and the Old School Presbyterian Churches. But their election did not result from any *right* those denominations had to be represented in the College Board. And the number of New School Presbyterians in the Board greatly preponderated over all other parties united, *as it was intended they should.* This continued to be the case for years, until after Mr. Blanchard became President, when he succeeded in bringing about a different state of things in the Board. The change he aimed at could never have been secured except from a change of sentiments on the part of some who were in the Board. Several trustees, who were ministers or elders in Presbyterian Churches when elected, and who were elected because they were Presbyterians, have since become very decided Congregationalists. They united with others who were Congregationalists when appointed, and under the leadership of Mr. Blanchard, have been laboring for the past few years to secure to Congregationalists a majority over all others in the Board, and thus to wrest the College from its founders. Mr. Blanchard was elected President of the College in 1845. At the time our thoughts were directed to him for this appointment, he was a Presbyterian minister of a Presbyterian Church in Cincinnati. Had we supposed then that he would become a Congregationalist when elected, he would never have been proposed as a candidate. Our former President, Rev. H. H. Kellogg, had been a Presbyterian. Mr. Blanchard, just before his election, stated to us that if he became our President, he would prefer to connect with an Association of Congregationalists, but at the same time he assured us that this was merely a matter of personal preference, and that he had no zeal for Congregationalism. This announcement gave many of us anxiety lest we should have trouble for the future, but our negotiations with him had then gone so far that it was thought best to complete them, and trust our peace to his honor. We soon found that we had introduced into the College and into the colony a man of unbounded hostility to the Presbyterian Church. Soon after he came here he stated that there ought to be only two denominations in the State—the Old School Presbyterians, and the Congregationalists. He has labored with all diligence to exterminate the Church which he has forsaken, and to build up the Congregational Church on its ruins. It was my misfortune to occupy a position on this ground which placed me directly in the way of his projects. The College had been founded by Presbyterians. The colony here had been planted by them. The Church first organized in the place, and which was the only one here for many years, had been organized purely Presbyterian. The region of country about, for a circuit of fifty miles, contained many Presbyterian Churches, and *not one* Congregational, when we came here. The whole region was not so much as nominally occupied by an Association at that time. Congregationalism was then hardly known in this part of Illinois. In the light of such facts, I did not feel it my duty to allow Mr. Blanchard to overturn all this work with no better object than that of the mere propagandist. I could not suffer the work of my own hands and that of my friends to be destroyed without at least a remonstrance. My opposition to Mr. Blanchard for these causes brought upon me a storm of wrath seldom equalled for violence, and which has raged against me for the last ten years. In 1848, a little more than two years after he became President, he addressed to me a letter, in which he distinctly presented to me this alternative, either to yield the Presbyterian interests here to Congregationalists, and secure their lasting gratitude for so doing, or else, by maintaining them, to meet with hostility and all its consequences. At that time there was in Galesburg a paper edited and published by a Presbyterian minister. Congregationalists were advised not to give it their support unless the editor would leave his Presbytery and join the Association. Those of them who were connected with the First Presbyterian Church, were advised, also, not to unite in calling or supporting a minister for that Church, unless the Presbyterian members, who were a large majority, would consent to settle a Congregationalist. The letter of Mr. Blanchard proposed these measures for my acceptance, and also the dissolution of Knox Presbytery, as the only grounds on which I could be allowed to live in peace. I quote a few sentences from that letter, to confirm my statements. The italics were made by Mr. Blanchard:

'Dec. 11, 1848. To Prof. Gale—Dear Brother: * * * Now you can take either one of three courses, in view of facts as they exist: 1st. You can quietly allow F—, (the Presbyterian editor) to join Association, and the Congregationalists to adopt his paper—allow a Congregational pastor to settle in this Church—our funds to Home Missions to go under Kirby's direction, to whose field we belong—merge Knox Presbytery in Peoria, or Schuyler, or one north—act as our daysman between us and Presbyterianism, in Chicago, and throughout the West and East—and make yourself, though not necessary to our existence as a College, yet necessary to our healthy, and in the highest degree, successful existence; or, 2nd. You can look on with comparative indifference; or, 3rd. You can prevent brother F— joining Association, and, (for in reason and nature it is the same thing,) prevent Congregational ministers adopting his paper. You can probably prevent for a time the peaceful settlement of a Congregational minister in this place. You can keep Knox Presbytery alive in its distinct existence. * * * I will suppose you to take the first or last of the above courses. If the first, in my humble judgment the following would be the result, to wit: You would be honored and courted as the representative of Presbyterianism, the good will of which is necessary to us, instead of being dreaded as the weakener of our home operations, newspaper, missions, etc. You would give the churches in this community peace. You would remove out of the way the only obstacle to our having a paper here which would make us respected at home and abroad. [The reader will bear in mind that this happy result would be secured, not by a new editor, but by a mere change, by the former editor, from Presbytery to Association.—GALE.] You will remove the only obstacle to our evangelical labors in this region. * * You would increase your own influence, however great it may now be in the Churches of Central Association, *and make yourself courted as the representative of Presbyterianism abroad, while you would not be dreaded as the representative of a disturbing force in our midst.* You would have, in short, all the advantages, from your principles, to yourself personally, which you can possibly have now, without that friction, which, by irritating the animal passions of men in the things of their religion, makes them desperate, and prone to every sort of extreme.

On the other hand, if you resolve to keep up the Presbyterian system in conjunction with the others, * * all this is not going to take place without engendering ill blood, and crimination among our people.   J. BLANCHARD.'

This proposition will, I trust, satisfy those who have heretofore doubted whether Mr. Blanchard ever openly and purposely made war upon Presbyterianism in this region. Here we have his own words. I did not, of course, feel disposed to yield long established and valuable rights, to one who was seeking with hostile efforts, to introduce a state of things among us, not known at the beginning. I refused to accept the *very flattering* offers made me—rejected the proffer of '*influence* in the churches of Central Association'—did not choose to occupy the position of 'representative of Presbyterianism *abroad*,' when all should be swept away at home—and, although I knew that, to Mr. Blanchard, our system was indeed 'a disturbing force,' yet I preferred to adhere to it, knowing that I was only maintaining what had been planted here by good men, and had been nurtured with many prayers. My steady adherence to Presbyterianism resulted, as Mr. Blanchard warned me it would, ' in irritating the animal passions ' of himself and his followers, ' in the things of their religion'—and this irritation, I have found to my cost, has made them all, and Mr. Blanchard in particular, '*desperate, and prone to every sort of extreme.*'

Justice to Knox College, as well as to myself, has seemed to demand this exposure of the true cause of all the wrath with which Mr. Blanchard has pursued me for so many years. It was because I would not suffer him, without opposition, to exterminate from this ground the long established interests of those by whom the College had been founded—the colony planted—and this whole region made prosperous and attractive.

The First Presbyterian Church in Galesburg was organized by myself, and by Bro. Noel, a committee of the Presbytery of Schuyler appointed for that purpose. It was organized as a purely Presbyterian Church, and continued such for about eight years. There was not, during those early years, the slightest departure from strict Presbyterianism in its polity or in its administration. When the Church was formed by direction of the Presbytery of Schuyler, a majority of that Presbytery were Old School men, and would not have organized and received into its connection a church that was not strictly Presbyterian. The only thing brought forward now, as evidence that the Church was not strictly Presbyterian at first, is the fact that sometimes the members remained after preparatory lectures, to witness the examination of candidates for membership by the Session, and were occasionally asked to express their opinion of the examination by vote. This practice I introduced myself, as I had been accustomed to it in New York; and it was never proposed as any part of Congregationalism. When the Second Presbyterian Church was organized by me in 1851, which was done for the express purpose of having a strictly Presbyterian Church, after the First Church had ceased to be such, I introduced the same practice, which certainly would not have been followed by that Church, as it was for a year or two, had it been supposed that it was in any manner an abandonment of strict Presbyterianism, and a concession to Congregationalism. The practice was adopted by me in New York, in place of the common method of 'propounding' members to the Church. It also gave the Church an opportunity of acquainting themselves fully with the Christian experience of those received into the Church. As I was pastor of the First Church in Galesburg for several years after its organization, I speak from personal knowledge, when I declare that from 1837 until 1845 it was strictly a Presbyterian Church. In 1845 a 'compromise' form of government was adopted, by which, while Presbyterian members retained all their rights, Congregational members received some privileges not before granted them. This was done as a concession on the part of the Church to its Congregational members, who were becoming somewhat numerous. Their method of gaining that concession was not honorable to their leaders. The Church had commenced building a house of worship. Rev. L. H. Parker, and some others, induced the Congregationalists to refuse to pay their subscriptions and taxes for the house, unless the Presbyterians would consent to modify the government of the Church. By this measure they secured the 'Compromise.' Having thus gained an 'entering wedge,' they have driven it perseveringly until the Church for several years past has been totally separated from all connection with the Presbyterian body. They, however, continue in possession of the property donated by the Presbyterian founders of the College to 'the Presbyterian Society' of Galesburg. To do this, they call themselves a 'Congregational Church,' by the name of 'The First Church of Christ,' and 'The First Presbyterian Society.' It is a Congregational Church and a Presbyterian Society, if any one knows how such a conglomerate is possible. The very fact that the Church is willing, for the sake of its property, to occupy such a position, which would be pronounced dishonorable, if not fraudulent, in any merely secular corporation or society, shows the character of the moulding spirits, the master minds, by whom that Church has so long been educated and controlled.

Since the removal of Mr. Blanchard from the Presidency of the College, the Congregationalists remain more numerous than Presbyterians in the Board. But with this they are not satisfied. They desire to become a majority over all others—and because disappointed in this, they have waged an incessant war upon the College during the last two years. If they cannot *rule,* they seem determined to *ruin.* That the Lord will overrule all this storm, and cause even 'the wrath of man to praise Him,' and to result in the future increased prosperity of the College, I have no doubt. The foundations of Knox College are embedded in too many prayers, and fervent desires to advance the cause of intelligence and pure religion, to be overturned by the ambition and sectarianism of such men as Mr. Blanchard and his followers.

GEO. W. GALE.

GALESBURG, Dec., 1859."

The next letter is from Mr. Silvanus Ferris, to whom the College is more indebted, for its success and present wealth, than to any other person except Mr. Gale. The property of the College was managed for a great many years by Mr. Ferris, as agent, and it is the unanimous opinion of the men in Galesburg best able to judge of the matter, that to his prudence and foresight the present wealth of the College is mainly due.

LETTER OF S. FERRIS.

"I was born in the year 1773, in the State of Connecticut, upon the borders of New York. When I was six years of age, my father removed his family into New York, in which State I continued to live until the year 1838, when I removed to Galesburg, in Illinois, where I have resided ever since. I was reared from childhood in the doctrines and under the influences of the Presbyterian Church. It was not until I had attained the age of manhood that I made a public profession of religion. I was then living in the town of Norway, New York. The Church with which I first united was in connection with Presbytery, according to the well-known 'Plan-of-Union.'

By this 'Plan,' Presbyterians and Congregationalists were able to unite in the same church without any relinquishment, on the part of either, of their denominational preferences. I would have preferred to unite with a purely Presbyterian Church, had there been one in the place. I often attended the meetings of Presbytery, as a Delegate from the Church, while I was one of its members.

I knew nothing of Congregational Associations while connected with this Church in Norway. The Church had no relations with any other body than the Presbytery.

After several years I removed to the town of Russia, New York, and there found a fully organized Presbyterian Church, with which I united, and in whose connection I remained several years, until my removal to Illinois.

When I came with my family to Galesburg, I joined the Presbyterian Church, which had just before been organized in that place. The Church was known as a regular, fully constituted Presbyterian Church at that time. I never heard, until several years afterward, any claims advanced in the Church, in behalf of Congregationalists. In 1845, the Constitution of the Church was modified, by adopting what is called the 'Compromise,' whereby Congregationalists were allowed some privileges they had never enjoyed before. Until the time of the 'Compromise,' the Church was, in the full sense, Presbyterian. In allowing to Congregationalists, as such, some privileges, it was not intended to take from Presbyterians any of their own. The Church retained its elders, and its connection with Presbytery, as before. In a few years, however, it was found that Congregational practices were undermining the original polity of the Church, and that Mr. Blanchard and others were determined to carry this on until the Church should lose all the distinct features of Presbyterianism. Finding that this result could not be prevented, without much confusion and strife in the Church, I proposed to the leading Presbyterian members of the Church a peaceable separation on our part from the others, and the organization of another fully Presbyterian Church. This was done in the year 1851, when the Second Presbyterian Church of Galesburg was formed.

These facts are mentioned by me, that it may be known how wholly unfounded is the statement, which has of late been given to the public, that I was formerly a Congregationalist. *I have never, in sentiment or in profession, been a Congregationalist in my whole life.*

I was well acquainted with the Rev. Geo. W. Gale at the time he originated the Plan whereby Knox College was founded and endowed. He was a relative of my wife, and for many years had been a warm friend of mine. The whole plan of the enterprise originated with him, as I know perfectly well. In 1835, he stated his plan to me, and from that time I engaged heartily with him in it, giving to it my time, and money, and personal efforts, as far as they were required. Mr. Gale was a Presbyterian. Rev. Mr. Waters, Rev. Mr. Kellogg, and others, who engaged in the enterprise, were also Presbyterians. At the time the land was bought and the College founded, every man who had subscribed money to aid in the work was, so far as I knew, a Presbyterian. I did not, at that time, know that there was even one Congregationalist among them all. I was one of the committee who purchased the lands. At Detroit, Mr. Thomas Simmons joined the rest of the committee, and traveled with us to Knox county. But not until long after that time did I know that he was a Congregationalist. *It was well understood, by all who knew anything about it, that this was a Presbyterian enterprise.* It was so understood after the College was founded, and no other claim has ever been advanced until within the last few years. It was the design of all who founded Knox College, to build up an institution which should be open to the youth of our country, without regard to denominational relations of any kind. At the same time, it was their design to transmit the control of their Institution mainly to men who would represent their own sentiments as Presbyterians. It was expected fully that while various denominations might be represented in the Board, yet the majority of Trustees would be men sympathizing, in ecclesiastical matters, with its founders. And therefore, for many years after the College was founded, a majority of its Trustees were Presbyterians. After Rev. Jonathan Blanchard became President of the College, it became apparent that he intended, if possible, to wrest it from Presbyterians, and give it into the hands of Congregationalists. For efforts of this kind, and for other reasons, he was, as early as 1849, on the point of being removed from the Board. The matter was adjusted, however, in a manner which led us to believe that no more causes of complaints of this kind would be given by him. The present large number of Congregationalists in the Board has not come through the appointment of so many of that denomination by the Board. Several of those who now are among the Congregational members of the Board, were Presbyterians by profession, when they were elected as Trustees, and they were elected because they were Presbyterians. They have since become Congregationalists, and have given their influence and votes to wrest the College from the hands of those *by whom they were appointed.* Against all such efforts I have, with other founders of the College, continually protested, AND DO PROTEST. If Congregationalists had founded Knox College, I should insist that it ought to be theirs. But as it was founded and endowed by Presbyterians, *it ought to be theirs.*

I have heard read with care, the pamphlet entitled, 'Rights of Congregationalists in Knox College,' published by order of the Congregational General Association of Illinois. From my own personal knowledge, I declare that publication to be false in all its essential points.   SILVANUS FERRIS.
GALESBURG, ILL., Dec. 10, 1859."

The next letter is from Professor N. H. Losey, who was one of the founders of the College, and who has been in its Faculty from its organization. His efforts have contributed largely to elevate the grade of scholarship in the College, and to make it, in that respect, truly an *alma mater* to its graduates. He was for eleven years the Treasurer, and for seventeen years the Secretary, of the College. No man is better versed in the early history of the College than he.

LETTER OF PROF. N. H. LOSEY.

" I was born in the State of New York, and was a teacher in the Oneida Institute in that State, when Rev. G. W. Gale originated the Plan for founding Knox College. I was well acquainted with Mr. Gale at that time, and also with a large number of those who became Subscribers to his Plan. I was myself a decided Presbyterian then, as I had been many years before, and have been always since. All the Subscribers by whom the College was founded were, so far as I then knew, Presbyterians. I afterward learned that one of them, Mr. Simmons, was a Congregationalist. The whole enterprise was well understood at that time to be exclusively Presbyterian. Their claim has never, to my knowledge, been questioned, until very recently. I have always opposed all measures which looked like an effort to transfer the control of the College to any other than Presbyterians. It has always been the desire of the founders, as our action clearly shows, to secure a fair representation of various denominations in the College Board. The recent efforts of Congregationalists to secure to themselves a majority of Trustees, and thus perpetuate the management of the College to their own denomination, *is in direct opposition to the well-known wishes of the founders*, and is justly characterized as an attempt at a gross usurpation. The present number of Congregational members in the Board is the result of a change of sentiment, on the part of several who were supposed to be Presbyterians in heart, as they were in profession, at the time they received their appointment.

I was present at the organization of the First Presbyterian Church in Galesburg, in 1837. It was voted unanimously that the church should be fully Presbyterian. I was elected one of its Elders at the time, which office I held until 1845, when the 'Compromise' was adopted. The Session administered the government of the Church, during all that time, as fully as in any Presbyterian Church in the world. The members of the Church often remained, after a preparatory lecture, to witness the examination of candidates for admission to the Church, and in some cases, especially when peculiar views were advanced by the candidate, respecting slavery, and other questions of reform, they were asked whether they were satisfied with the sentiments expressed. But the church never, previous to the 'Compromise,' voted upon the reception or dismission of members, or in any manner departed from the usages common in the Presbyterian Church.

N. H. LOSEY.

DECEMBER, 1859."

The letter that follows is from Rev. Hiram H. Kellogg, a Presbyterian minister, well known in the State of New York. He was the first one who subscribed to Mr. Gale's Plan. He became the first President of the College in 1839, and remained in that office until 1845, when he resigned. He has always cherished a deep interest in the College, and has looked with no little alarm upon the efforts of Congregationalists to secure for themselves its control. His letter was written *before the removal* of Mr. Blanchard from the Presidency, and had reference to that result.

LETTER OF EX-PRESIDENT H. H. KELLOGG.

"MARSHALL, ONEIDA Co., May 5, 1857.

* * * As to ecclesiastical relations, you know I am not a strong sectarian. I am of conviction and choice, a moderate New

School Presbyterian; but I have no sympathy with denominational strife, and no desire for denominational aggrandizement. If I was a Congregationalist, I should be a moderate one, and *if so*, I think I should still be, *as I now am, of opinion that Knox College should be under a leading Presbyterian influence.* I would have the two denominations represented in its Boards of counsel and instruction. *Yet I would have the Presbyterian a leading interest.* My reason for this is not as a matter of choice, or elective affinity, but of simple justice and right. *It was so projected—so understood from the beginning.* Its main parents, authors of its existence, *were Presbyterian*, and their whole action, including the plan for a Theological School, shows this. *Mutatis mutandis*, if the Institution, in these respects, had been as much Congregational as it has been Presbyterian, I should say as decidedly that its leading influences should continue to be Congregational. * * *I would have the President a Presbyterian, as a matter of principle.*
H. H. KELLOGG."

The reader has not forgotten the part taken by Mr. T. B. Jervis, as one of the Exploring Committee, in securing the present location for the College. Mr. Jervis was a Subscriber, and, soon after the College was founded, became a minister in the Presbyterian Church, in which connection he still remains. His letter, which follows, will show what were his expectations as to the denominational character of the College which he labored so diligently to establish.

LETTER OF REV. T. B. JERVIS.

"NEWPORT, NEW YORK, Aug. 10, 1858.

* * * You will remember that I was appointed one, of a committee of three, to explore the central part of Illinois, for the purpose of ascertaining the most suitable location of such an Institution. With regard to the Institution, I can only say, that while it was not my supposition that it was to be of a sectarian character, *I did think that it was to be placed under decidedly Presbyterian auspices.* I knew that all the friends of the enterprise, with whom I was personally acquainted, were members of the Presbyterian Church.
T. B. JERVIS."

Mr. Thomas Gilbert was also a member of the Exploring Committee, and in his reports to the Prudential Committee indicated so nearly the present site of the College, that the Purchasing Committee came immediately to Knoxville, five miles from Galesburg, in the full expectation of finding in the neighborhood, as they did, a suitable location.

LETTER OF THOS. GILBERT.

"I certify that I was one of the original Subscribers to a Plan for founding an institution of learning in the West, agreeably to a Plan which was drawn up and advocated by Rev. G. W. Gale; and that I was appointed and served as one of an Exploring Committee, which was sent out to find a suitable location for the said institution. The Plan of the enterprise was drawn by Mr. Gale. *I always understood that it was to be strictly a Presbyterian Institution.* The enterprise resulted in the establishment of Knox College.

KNOXVILLE, July 5, 1859." THOMAS GILBERT.

Benjamin P. Johnson, Esq., now residing at Albany, New York, is widely known in this country as the Secretary of the New York State Agricultural Society. He was a Subscriber to the Plan by which Knox College was built up, and aided by his counsels in securing the result. This is his testimony:

LETTER OF B. P. JOHNSON.

"ALBANY, August 11, 1858.

I knew well the early history of the Galesburg effort. Knowing, as I did, the men engaged in the enterprise, I was not a little surprised at the assurance with which it has been put forth, that Congregationalists are the men who should have the control of this great work. *Certainly in its inception they had little or nothing to do with it.* It appears that the great object has been to avail themselves of other men's labors to further their own, I fear, merely sectarian schemes. I trust, however, God in His providence has opened a way of deliverance, etc. * * If my life should be spared, I hope to visit Galesburg, and witness what has been done by those godly men with whom I once took counsel, and whose success has ever been dear to me. B. P. JOHNSON."

Jeremiah Holt, Esq., of Cleveland, Ohio, was a Subscriber, and thus writes to Rev. Mr. Gale:

LETTER OF J. HOLT.

"CLEVELAND, Aug. 18, 1858.

I was greatly interested in the enterprise which you originated in the State of New York, from which Knox College has resulted, and have deeply sympathized with those who have sought its prosperity, during its whole history. I was an Elder of the First Presbyterian Church of Watertown, New York, at the time when the meetings were held in reference to the Plan you proposed for the establishment of institutions at the West, and was the Secretary of the meeting at Whitesboro', on the 19th of August, 1835. *Those who felt an interest in the matter and who subscribed to the fund were members of the Presbyterian Church, so far as I knew.* And while none of us contemplated a sectarian institution, *it was understood that as you were a Presbyterian, this would be the general character of the College.* I shall hope and pray for its future prosperity with much of the feeling that I first cherished in its behalf.

JEREMIAH HOLT."

LETTER OF REV. J. FROST.

Rev. John Frost, another Subscriber, who is not now living, was widely known for many years in Central New York, as an efficient and devoted Presbyterian minister. In a letter written by him to Mr. Gale, dated "Elmira, June 29, 1837," a year and a half after the College was founded, and a few days only after the famous "Exscinding Acts" of the majority of the General Assembly of the Presbyterian Church, he used this language: "I rejoice that you have the prospect of doing so much good in connection with your associates as may reasonably be expected from the Plan if carried out. As *we* are likely to be cut off from most of the Colleges and Theological Seminaries *which are controlled by Presbyterians*, we must be awake *to the establishment of new ones*," etc. In other words, Mr. Frost rejoiced in the prospective success of Knox College, because it would be a "new one" in the place of those from which its founders had been driven, and which had always been "*controlled by Presbyterians.*" He expected Knox College to supply the place, in part, of those they had lost, and to be "controlled by Presbyterians," as they had been.

Thomas G. Frost, Esq., a Trustee of the College, and a prominent lawyer, living in Galesburg, is a son of Rev. John Frost, and assures the writer that the sentiments of his father were correctly represented in the language of the letter just quoted. He also stated in writing, before he removed to Galesburg, "that when Mr. Gale formed the Plan of founding a colony and establishing a College in Galesburg, Illinois, his father took a deep interest in the scheme, manifested at the time by contributing to its funds, and subsequently by constant and earnest countenance and support, until the day of his death. His anticipations of the results of the enterprise were of the most ardent and enthusiastic character. His hope rested not only upon the vast and enlightened Christian influence secured by the institution thus established, but also upon the tried Christian fidelity, experience and wisdom *of the founder* of the enterprise, *and which*, under the smiles of Providence, *he fondly trusted would continue*, unimpaired by alienation, or distrust, *to guide and control its destinies.*"

Rev. Phineas Camp, now in the Presbytery of Utica, a Subscriber, and a warm friend of the College enterprise, thus writes:

LETTER OF REV. P. CAMP.

"I hereby certify that I have known the Rev. G. W. Gale for many years. A year or two before he commenced operations toward founding a literary institution at the West he communicated his design and the plan to me. I was in favor of the plan, and subsequently put in funds to aid in its establishment. It was regarded as an enterprise of Mr. Gale, originating wholly with him. *Those who united with him were chiefly of the Presbyterian denomination*, and *it was considered a Presbyterian enterprise.* Its founders and friends in this region have looked upon it with great interest, and I believe would exceedingly regret any effort *to divert* it from its original purpose and regard it as *an act of injustice to its founders.*   PHINEAS CAMP,

SEPT. 15, 1855.   *Minister in connection with the Presbytery of Utica.*"

Sidney Rice, Esq., and his sister, Miss Araminta P. Rice, were both Subscribers to the plan for founding Knox College. Mr. Rice thus writes in behalf of himself and also of his sister:

LETTER OF S. RICE.

"I was a Subscriber in 1835 to a plan drawn up by Rev. G. W. Gale, for establishing a College and other literary institutions in the

West. That plan resulted in founding Knox College, Illinois. My sister, Miss A. P. Rice, was also a Subscriber to the same plan. We both took farm lands, in accordance with the plan, equal in value to the amount of our subscriptions. These lands we returned to the College when it was found that they would be of more value to it than the money. *We were Presbyterians*, and were members of the First Presbyterian Church, Dr. Beman's, in Troy, N. Y., at the time the College was founded. *The enterprise was understood by us to be exclusively one of Presbyterians.* We did not know that Congregationalists had any part in the work of founding the College. It was the intention of those who engaged in the work, to found a College which should be liberal, and which should offer its advantages for education alike to all. But we never supposed that the College would be controlled by any other denomination of Christians than *the one to which the founders belonged.* An attempt by any party whatever, to wrest the College from the control of Presbyterians, would be regarded by us as *in open conflict* with the expectation of those by whom it was founded.

SIDNEY RICE.

CINCINNATI, OHIO, March 3, 1860."

STATEMENT OF THOMAS SIMMONS.

Mr. Thomas Simmons, the Congregational Subscriber, in personal conversation with the writer of this, somewhat more than a year ago, *admitted fully that all the founders of the College were Presbyterians except himself.* He justified the attempts of Congregationalists to secure the control of the College, on the ground that the Congregational denomination was more numerous in this part of Illinois, as he supposed, than the Presbyterian, and the strongest party ought to rule. This sort of logic may answer at a Congregational church meeting, but it will hardly avail to settle questions involving the rights of founders of Colleges. The views of Mr. Simmons are also stated by his son-in-law, Mr. E. S. Hitchcock, an Elder in the Second Presbyterian Church in Galesburg, in the following language:

"I am the son-in-law of Mr. Thomas Simmons, one of the founders of Knox College. Mr. Simmons has admitted, in conversations on the subject with me, that *the College originated with Presbyterians.* During the present week, in reply to a question by me, with direct reference to this point, he stated distinctly that so far as he knew, *all the Subscribers,* by whom the College was founded, *were Presbyterians, except himself.*

Before I removed to Galesburg among its early settlers, I was well acquainted with the history of the enterprise for founding a College here, and with some of its founders, and I understood that it was a work undertaken by Presbyterians. I have never heard any other claim advanced, until within a few years.

January 2, 1860." E. S. Hitchcock.

The Rev. L. H. Loss was deeply interested in Mr. Gale's plan, although not a Subscriber, and aided in drafting the plan, while he was pastor of a Presbyterian church at New York Mills. As he is well known throughout this State and elsewhere, his testimony is here given, as follows:

LETTER OF REV. L. H. LOSS.

"In reference to what I know of the origin and founding of Knox College, I have to say that I was acquainted with this enterprise from its commencement. In the summer of 1834, Rev. Geo. W. Gale, with whom I had been intimately acquainted for many years, called on me at my house at the New York Mills, while I was pastor of the Presbyterian church there, and laid before me a plan which he had conceived, of founding an institution of learning somewhere in the West. We had repeated conferences on the subject, and at his request, in accordance with his suggestions, I made a draft of the plan, which, after some modifications, was adopted, and is the Plan upon which the Galesburg Colony and Knox College, of Illinois, was founded. Although not a Subscriber, I was deeply interested in the success of the enterprise, and gave to it most cordially, all the aid I could. I was personally acquainted with most of the ministers who embarked in it. They were members, with me, of the Oneida (now Utica) Presbytery. I was also well acquainted with many of the Elders and other gentlemen who were the original Subscribers of the Company. I was present at the meeting of the Subscribers held in Whitesboro', N. Y., in January, 1836. At that meeting the committees all reported—the College and town were named—the Trustees chosen, and the farming lands distributed. *Up to this time, and as far as I know, for many years after, the Presbyterian paternity and character of the enterprise were undisputed and undoubted.*

L. H. Loss."

The reader must be fully satisfied by this time, that the Subscribers who founded Knox College were Presbyterians, and that they intended to transmit its control to Presbyterians. To multiply testimony of the same kind as the foregoing, would add nothing to the completeness of the proof. We have here the testimony of the one Congregational Subscriber, as well as that of others. All state exactly the same thing concerning the denominational character of the men by whom the College was founded.

Here then, it is settled by the founders of the College, that they intended to transmit the control of the College to Presbyterians; and that the supremacy of Congregationalists in its control would be a usurpation, in direct opposition to the rights and wishes of those founders. And yet, during the lifetime of those founders, in total disregard of all their intentions, and in conflict with all their early acts, Mr. Blanchard and his friends had almost accomplished that usurpation; and because the majority of the College Board, composed of men of four different denominations, and of others who are connected as members with none, would not suffer them to consummate their designs, they have raised a great outcry, and thereby have greatly embittered a large part of the Congregational body against the College. But Truth will spread, and when the public come to understand that Presbyterians founded, and also endowed Knox College, they will see that the war waged against it during the last two years, by certain Congregationalists, has scarcely its parallel in sectarian injustice and outrage. The Congregational body will condemn at last the great wrong which has been perpetrated under its name.

It ought here to be stated, that no one has ever pretended to claim, until recently, that the College was not founded by Presbyterians, and of right belonged to them. Plots enough have been carried on, for several years, to wrest it from them; but only since the removal of Mr. Blanchard, and the consequent defeat of those plots, has any one had the boldness to assert that it was mainly founded and endowed by Congregationalists. Mr. Blanchard well knew it to be a Presbyterian College, when he became its President, and on that account felt it necessary to assure the Board, that in connecting himself with the Congregational body, he had no special zeal in that direction, which need alarm them. In the year 1844, the Board made application for aid from the Society for Collegiate and Theological Education at the West. Mr. Gale, who was instructed to make this application, in a letter written at the time, to a leading Director of that Society, among other reasons why aid should be granted, stated particularly the evangelical character, and consequent religious importance of the College, in these words: " *We are Presbyterians* in connection with the Constitutional Assembly. While we feel it a duty as Christians to cultivate friendly and kind relations with evangelical Christians of all denominations, and particularly with our Congregational brethren, with whom we are so closely allied in everything but church polity, we are by education and *deliberate preference* Presbyterians."

The application for aid was not granted at that time, the Society having engaged in a strenuous effort to build up Illinois College, and also wishing to found a new College at Davenport, Iowa. In 1847, Mr. Blanchard, who was then President of the College, was directed to renew the application, which he did. He presented a written report of his efforts to the Board, in which he uses this language, which is certainly very remarkable, if the College was then understood by him to be Congregational. " Knowing," Mr. Blanchard says, " that there is, in many parts of the East, a great and growing dissatisfaction, that funds *given by Eastern Congregationalists*, should be applied in the West to the promotion of *other principles of church government* than those of *the donors*, I *yet* felt it my duty, being *myself* a Congregationalist, to inform those concerned, of my intention, in case Knox College was rejected by the College Society, to appeal to Eastern Congregationalists against the decision." Here Mr. Blanchard clearly states that any " funds given by Eastern Congregationalists " to Knox College, at that time, would have been given " to the promotion of other principles of church government than those of the donors." We have here his own written testimony that the College was not then a Congregational institution. In the same report, Mr. Blanchard stated that " when our application was argued before the Board of the College Society, Dr. Bacon strongly insisted that it was necessary to take up Knox College, to prevent the appeal which would be made *to the rising spirit* of Congregationalism at the East." In other words, Dr. Bacon apprehended that this PRESBYTERIAN College, unless protected by the sheltering wing of the College Society, might, through the appeal of its own President, become a prey to " the rising spirit of Congregationalism at the East." Happy would it have been for Knox College, had Mr. Blanchard been as effectually prevented, since that time, from making his appeal, not to secure aid for the College, but to arouse prejudice against it, to "the rising spirit of Congregationalism" *at the West.*

THE COLLEGE BOARD.

When the College was founded, in January, 1836, a temporary Board of ten members was appointed, of whom, all but two were founders. Eight of the whole number were Presbyterians, and two were Congregationalists. During the year, Mr. Matthew Chambers, a Congregationalist, was added. In February, 1837, the Legislature of Illinois granted a Charter, in which the following eleven persons were named as the Corporate Board:

Rev. John Waters, Presbyterian.
" Geo. W. Gale, "
Nehemiah West, " Elder.
Parnach Owen, " "
R. H. Hurlburt, " "
N. H. Losey, "
Geo. W. Wright, Non-Professor, afterward Pres. Elder.
John G. Sanborn, Episcopalian.
Matthew Chambers, Congregationalist.
Erastus Swift, "
Thomas Simmons, "

The two last named Congregationalists, before the Board was organized, became members of the Presbyterian Church in Galesburg. Mr. M. Chambers removed from Vermont to Knoxville, the town adjoining Galesburg, in 1836, and united with the Presbyterian Church there, of which he was a member *when he was appointed* in the Charter. *He became a ruling Elder* in that Church *before* the Board had organized, and continued to hold the office during the five years he remained in the Knoxville Church. He then removed to Galesburg, and again for many years was an Elder in the Presbyterian Church there. He now, however, chooses to regard all those professions, and solemn oaths as an officer in the Presbyterian Church, as no true index to his real sentiments, and so he is here accounted as a Congregationalist. The persons enumerated in the above list as Presbyterians were all sincerely such then, and have continued to be such until now.

Thus it will be seen the corporate Board consisted of eight men taken from the Presbyterian Church and connection, and two from the Congregational. Seven of the number were *in sentiment* Presbyterians and three were Congregationalists.

THE COLLEGE BOARD.

The following list includes all the additions that have ever been made to the original corporate Board:

In 1837, Wm. Holyoke, Presbyterian Elder, In Cincinnati and in Galesburg.
" "   Peter Butler, Baptist.
" "   Silvanus Ferris, Presbyterian.
" 1838, Rev. H. H. Kellogg, " President and *ex officio* Trustee.
" 1843, Hon. James Knox, Not Ch. Member. Resigned soon.
" 1845, Rev. Aratus Kent, Presbyterian. Did not accept.
" "   "   Horatio Foot, Congregationalist.
" "   "   Flavel Bascom, Presbyterian.
" "   "   Milton Kimball, "
" "   Eli Farnham, " Elder.
" "   James Bunce, "
" "   James Bull, "
" "   Rev. H. H. Kellogg, " Res'd Presidency, elected Trus.
" "   "   J. Blanchard, Congregationalist. Pres't and Trust.
" 1848, Hon. James Knox, Not Ch. Member.
" "   C. S. Colton, Congregationalist.
" "   S. F. Dolbear, Presbyterian.
" "   Levi Sanderson, Congregationalist.
" 1850, Hon. O. H. Browning, Not Ch. Member.
" "   Marcus B. Osborne, Presbyterian Elder.
" "   Wm. E. Withrow, "   "
" "   Levi S. Stanley, "   "
" "   Rev. S. G. Wright, Congregationalist.
" 1852, Wm. J. Phelps, "
" "   Rev. W. E. Holyoke, "
" 1856, Caleb M. Pomroy, Baptist.
" 1858, Thos. G. Frost, Presbyterian.
" "   Rev. H. Curtis, D.D., " Pres't and Trust.

In the above list, Mr. Eli Farnham is named as an Elder in a Presbyterian Church, at the time he was elected a Trustee. He had been a member of a Presbyterian Church more than eight years before that election, and during several of those years had been an Elder, which office he continued to hold long after he became a Trustee of the College. He is now a Congregationalist, and claims that he was at that time also in sentiment a Congregationalist. Perhaps he was, but when men have been for years members of the Presbyterian Church, and have held office as Elders in that Church, and have been appointed as Trustees in the College while thus connected, and *because they were supposed to be, what they professed to be—Presbyterians*, they cannot reasonably ask to be allowed to credit their election to the benefit of the Congregational body. Mr. Farnham was elected to the Board because he was supposed to be a Presbyterian. Yet, from the fact that all in the above list were *in sentiment*, as well as in profession, what they are there stated to have been, except Mr. Farnham, he will in what follows be reckoned among the Congregationalists. Thus that denomination is credited with *all who have ever* claimed to be in sympathy with it when elected to the Board, even although they *professed* to be Presbyterians, and were elected on account of their profession.

The above list shows that twenty-eight persons, including the Presidents, have been elected to the Board since its organization under the charter. Of this number, fifteen were honest Presbyterians when elected, and eight were Congregationalists, including among them one Presbyterian Elder. The list shows that previous to the election of Mr. Blanchard, in 1845, a period of more than eight years, *nine* Presbyterians had been elected, and exactly TWO Congregationalists, *one* of whom was a Presbyterian Elder! The list shows what changes were wrought in the Board by Mr. Blanchard, after his election. In the corporate Board, it has been shown, were seven true Presbyterians, and three Congregationalists, including among *them*, also, one who for years from that time was a Presbyterian Elder. Previous to the election of Mr. Blanchard as President, there had been appointed to the Board, including corporate members, sixteen Presbyterians, and five Congregationalists, two of whom professed to be Presbyterians. Including charter members, there have been thirty-nine Trustees, of whom twenty-two were sincere Presbyterians, and eleven were Congregationalists. Two of the Trustees were never members of any church, but both of them were when elected, as they have continued to be ever since, supporters of the Presbyterian Church.

The reader thus sees that previous to the election of Mr. Blanchard to the Presidency of the College, the Board was almost wholly Presbyterian. Indeed, of the Congregationalists elected during that period *only three* were at the time of their election *professedly* Congregationalists. In the foregoing statements, that denomination has been credited with all the Presbyterian members and Elders, whom they have ever claimed as being, in personal preference, their own.

It has so happened in the history of the Board, that only one of all the places filled by Congregationalists had ever been vacated, previous to the removal of Mr. Blanchard, while a large number of places filled by Presbyterians have been made vacant by the removal from the State or by the death of the incumbents. Notwithstanding this fact, however, the Congregational party in the Board would be a small minority at the present time, if it were composed of those only *who were elected as Congregationalists.* The present strength of that party has been caused by the fact that several Trustees who were by profession Presbyterians when elected, and *who were elected to represent Presbyterian interests,* have since become Congregationalists. Rev. Flavel Bascom had been for many years previous to his election, a prominent Presbyterian minister in this State. *He was elected to the Board as a Presbyterian.* He now leads the Congregational party in the Board. Mr. Eli Farnham was an Elder in the Presbyterian church when elected a Trustee of the College, and *he was elected because he professed to be a Presbyterian.* He is now a Congregationalist. Other members, who were professed Presbyterians when elected, are now claimed as Congregationalists. They were elected as Presbyterians and not as Congregationalists. They have a right to change their denominational relations if they desire to do so. *But they have no right to carry over with them to the Congregational body rights which were intrusted to them as Presbyterians.* This they have done. They have taken advantage of their own change of relations to invest the Congregational body with rights in Knox College, which were never granted to that body by its founders, or by its Board of Trustees. And because the Board will not allow them to complete their purpose, which they had so nearly accomplished, they now labor through the General Association of Illinois, and through the Congregational Herald of Chicago, to injure the prosperity of the College. They complain that their rights in the College as Congregationalists have been invaded. To several of those who thus complain, the College never intrusted any rights *as Congregationalists.* The rights now in their hands were committed to them as Presbyterians. Moreover, what rights have they lost? Mr. Blanchard is the only man of their number who has been removed. Had they *a right* to retain him as President of the College against the majority of the Board? It is time the public understood that this outcry, about the loss of rights in the College by Congregationalists, is wholly without foundation in facts. It would be well, also, not merely for Knox College, but for other Institutions and Societies in our land, to have the question clearly settled, as early as possible, whether Congregationalists, who were once members of Presbyterian churches, intend to claim for their own denomination all rights and interests which were committed to them when they were Presbyterians. That they are justified in doing this, seems at present to be the doctrine indorsed by the General Association of Illinois. If that doctrine is to prevail in that body, it is time it was known, at least by the Presbyterian church.

THE FIRST CHURCH IN GALESBURG.

A church was organized by the Christian settlers of Galesburg in the early part of 1837. That church was, as its own records state, "fully Presbyterian." From its organization until 1845, it was as entirely Presbyterian in all its polity as it is possible for any church to be. It was in connection with Presbytery, and its government was administered exclusively by its Session. This is asserted by all those now living, who were among its leading members at that time. It is clearly proved by its records. Professor Losey, who was one of its Elders from its organization until the "Compromise," in 1845, asserts that the church was during all that time wholly Presbyterian. The same thing is proved by the "Compromise," which granted to the church, as a concession to Congregationalists, the privilege of voting with the Session upon the reception of members and, in certain cases, of trying members accused of wrong doing. The fact that these privileges were granted as a "Compromise" shows that they were not previously held as an original right.

That it was Presbyterian is evident from the fact shown in its own records, that more than two-thirds of those who first united with the church, and whose vote determined its polity, were Presbyterians. The "Rights of Congregationalists" asserts that from a very early date the church *records*, whose language it professes to quote, state that members were *always* received by "vote of the church and session." How far from correct the assertion is will appear from the following certificate of Mr. Norman Churchill, the present clerk of the church and session: "I certify that until the time of the Compromise in 1845, the church records *do not state in a single instance* that members were received into the church by 'vote of the church and session.'—N. CHURCHILL." The writer of this knows from a careful examination of the records of that church that there is no evidence in them of any practice not strictly Presbyterian before the adoption of the Compromise. The recent attempt to prove that from the beginning the Church was semi-Congregational is contradicted by its own records—by its early members—and by the very terms of the Compromise. When that Church was organized there was not a Congregational Church within fifty miles of Galesburg, nor a Congregational Association in all this region of Illinois ; while at the same time, Presbyterian Churches were scattered over the whole region, and the Church was formed by a Committee of Schuyler Presbytery, within whose bounds the colony had settled. Only a little more than two years ago Mr. Blanchard published a letter in the Galesburg Newspaper in which he confirms the above statements. In that letter he says : " You remember when the *First Church in Galesburg* and when Churches in Peoria, Farmington, Canton, Virgil, Henderson, Lafayette and Victoria, were all *New School Presbyterian Churches.* They have *changed* their *polity* without even a split. There are now no New School Presbyterian Churches in either of the above places except in this city." The world grows wise with rapid strides ! Two years ago Mr. Blanchard was certain that all here could " remember when the First Church in Galesburg was a New School Presbyterian Church"—and that it had become Congregational by a *change* from its original polity ! Within these two short years, however, the whole Congregational Association of this State, including Mr. Blanchard, have discovered that this Church was never a New School Presbyterian Church in its polity.

The church adopted its Compromise, in 1845, a few weeks before Mr. Blanchard became President of the College. They were led to do this through the efforts of Rev. L. H. Parker, a Congregationalist, who acknowledged at the time, that the " Compromise " was a magnanimous sacrifice on the part of the church to its Congregational members. It was a *sacrifice* in the largest sense, for the advantage then secured by Congregationalists was used as a means of securing still greater advantages, until at last the Church has become wholly Congregational. The change, however, was not secured from an original preference on the part of the majority of its members for the Congregational polity, but from the notion that all the sins of American Slavery would be charged upon that particular Church, if they did not " come out " and " separate " themselves from the Presbyterian General Assembly. In 1851, the Church petitioned the whole Presbytery with which they were connected to separate from the Assembly solely on account of Slavery. In 1853, they resolved to send no more delegates to Presbytery until that body would comply with their former request. In 1855 they voted themselves out of all connection with the Presbytery, because their former petition had not been granted, and for no other reason. In 1856 they dropped the word Presbyterian from their name. Their present position and polity is shown in the following language of the printed Manual of the Church published about two years ago: "*Its Church polity is that of independence.* All power resides within the Church. It recognizes no right of appeal, by any of its members, from itself to any ecclesiastical body or bodies." This is its present polity. In the light of this declaration of the Church, consider the following facts: The Presbyterian founders of the College donated building lots to the "Presbyterian Society of Galesburg." This Church received those lots, being then the "Presbyterian Church of Galesburg." They have now changed their name and call themselves the "First Church of Christ in Galesburg;" and they have separated entirely from the Presbyterian body in this country—have changed their polity radically—and declare their "Church polity to be that of independence." Yet they retain possession of the property given to the "Presbyterian Society," and they do it through the following miserable fiction: They call themselves a "Congregational Church"—independent in polity, by the name of "The First Church of Christ" *and* "The First Presbyterian Society." Henceforth there will be needed a new chapter in Ecclesiastical History, showing the *rationale* of a single body constituting at once both a Congregational Church and a Presbyterian Society! The "developement" of that Church into its present position is mainly due to Mr. Blanchard. The early records of the Church and the "Compromise" are here published, that all may judge for themselves, whether or not the Church first established here was "fully Presbyterian."

CHURCH RECORDS.

(1.) "FEBRUARY 15, 1837.

The professors of religion in Galesburg met agreeably to appointment, at the School House in Henderson Grove, for the purpose of conferring on the subject of forming a Church in this place. The meeting was opened with prayer. Ministers present: Rev. John

Waters, who presided, and Rev. Geo. W. Gale, both from the Presbytery of Oneida, New York.

"After free conversation and prayer, it was *Resolved* unanimously that it is expedient, as soon as practicable, to form a Church in this place. 2d, It was *Resolved*, that it is expedient, *for the sake* of becoming better acquainted with each other's Christian character, to have each one give an account of the reason *of* his hope—those who present letters, as well as those who design for the first time to make a profession of religion. The meeting was interesting and harmonious. Adjourned, to meet in the same place on Friday of the present week. Closed with prayer."

(2.)

"FEBRUARY 17, 1837.

The congregation met agreeably to adjournment, and was opened with prayer. Members present as at previous meeting. Thirty-one persons presented letters from different churches in New York and New England, and were examined agreeably to the resolution on experimental religion. The meeting was deeply solemn and interesting. Closed with prayer."

(3.)

"FEBRUARY 21, (Evening).

Met for the purpose of continuing the business of the former meeting, which was spent, as were several other evenings, in receiving letters and hearing the Christian experience of such, and of examining those who desired for the first time to connect themselves with the Church."

"SATURDAY, FERRUARY 25.

Met again at the School House. Meeting opened with prayer. Present: Rev. J. Waters, who presided, Rev. Geo. W. Gale, and Rev. Mr. Noel, of the Presbytery of Schuyler, Ill., who had been appointed by his Presbytery to aid in the formation of a Church in this place. The examination of candidates for Church fellowship was continued and finished, when addresses were made by the ministering brethren, and a Confession of Faith and Covenant presented for consideration. After explanations and remarks in regard to the Confession of Faith and Covenant, the same was unanimously approved. It was resolved that the Lord's Supper be administered on the ensuing Sabbath, and all who had presented letters and been examined with a view to their making a profession of religion, be received and required publicly to give their assent to the Confession of Faith and Covenant. Closed with prayer."

(4.)

"SABBATH, FEBRUARY 26.

It being inconvenient for the Rev. Mr. Noel to be present, the Rev. Geo. W. Gale preached in the morning. The afternoon was occupied in adopting the Confession of Faith and Covenant, and in the administration of baptism and the Lord's Supper." (Here follow some remarks about the solemnity of the occasion.) "Sixty-four united with the Church by letter, and eighteen on confession—making eighty-two in all that united on this occasion."

(5.)
"WEDNESDAY, APRIL 5, 1837.

The Church members met at the School House agreeably to appointment, and the meeting was opened with prayer. Present: Rev. John Waters and Geo. W. Gale. After remarks by the ministering brethren present, and prayer, *it was Resolved* UNANIMOUSLY *that it is expedient to organize the Church* FULLY *as Presbyterian,* and to choose three Elders and two Deacons at the present time. The following persons were then chosen Elders and Deacons by ballot: Nehemiah West, Nehemiah H. Losey, and John Kendall, Elders; and Thomas Simmons, and Abel Goodell, Deacons. Closed with prayer."

(6.)
"SABBATH, APRIL 9, 1837.

The above mentioned officers, viz: N. H. Losey and John Kendall were ordained to the office of *Ruling Elders,* and with N. West, who had been ordained previously, were installed in office; and Abel Goodell, who was ordained as Deacon, and Thomas Simmons, who had before been ordained, were also installed in office.

"A Sermon was preached on the occasion, and the questions put to the candidates and Church by Rev. Geo. W. Gale, and the prayer offered by the Rev. John Waters. The Church was *then* declared organized by the name of the 'PRESBYTERIAN CHURCH of Galesburg.'"

"*Session* met after the congregation was dismissed, and designated John Kendall as their delegate to the Presbytery of Schuyler, with the request that this Church be taken under the care of that Presbytery."

"APRIL 25, 1837.

Session met. Rev. Geo. W. Gale reported that he and John Kendall had attended a meeting of the Schuyler Presbytery, and that this Church was received under its care." (Members received.)

COMPROMISE.

"At a meeting of the *Presbyterian Church* of Galesburg, held at the Academy, June 25, 1845, called for the purpose of uniting upon a Plan of Union, to meet the preferences of those in the Church who were partial to the Congregational as well as the Presbyterian form of government, Motion made by Mr. C. S. Colton, that the Plan of Union adopted by the General Assembly in 1801, be the basis of a Plan to be adopted by this Church. A Plan was then presented as follows:

1st. That no member shall hereafter be received into this Church except at a Church meeting, when every member may have an equal voice in the case.

[2nd and 3rd articles relate to alternation in office of Elders and Deacons.]

4th. That when any member shall come under censure of the Church, such member may elect whether to be tried by the Session, or by the adult members of the whole Church, and have the same right of appeal as granted by the Presbyterian and Congregational Churches in their respective bodies.

5th. That the Church may be represented in Association and Presbytery."

These articles were adopted July 5th, 1845.

"I hereby certify that I have for many years kept the records of the Church and Session of the 'First Church of Christ,' formerly the 'First Presbyterian Church' in Galesburg; and that the foregoing are true copies of the records, embracing the minutes of all the meetings held before and up to the complete organization of the Church. I further certify, that until the time of the 'Compromise,' in 1845, of which the above is a true copy, the Church records do not state in a single instance that members were received into the Church by 'vote of the Church and Session.'

N. CHURCHILL,

DEC. 31st, 1859.   *Clerk of Church and Session.*"

THE PRESIDENCY.

The causes which secured the present strength of the Congregational party in the Board have been spoken of already. By death, and by removals from the State, and by a change in denominational relations, the Board, which consists of twenty-five members, was during a few years preceding the removal of Mr. Blanchard, divided in respect to Church connections as follows: Twelve were Congregationalists, nine were Presbyterians, one was an Episcopalian, one was a Baptist, and two were not members of any church. The Congregationalists thus needed only one more member to constitute them a majority of the whole Board. They had in fact been an acting majority for three or four successive years preceding 1857, owing to the absence of other members. This had encouraged them to hope that soon the entire control of the College would be secured by their party. Mr. Blanchard was especially desirous of securing this result, because he well knew that he was so objectionable to the majority of the Board, that whenever they should all meet, he would be requested to resign.

Many serious objections existed against him, as President of the

College. Some of those who have been loudest in their denunciation of the members of the Board who removed him from office, are known to have expressed freely, before that act, the opinion that his peculiar characteristics as a man, and the strong prejudices against him, which were wide-spread through the State, rendered him unfit to be at the head of the College. Even Rev. Dr. Beecher had expressed such an opinion. It was a fact presented at the meeting of the Board, when Mr. Blanchard was requested to resign, that during the previous five or six years, the College had made no advance in its average number of students, and that, too, when the population of this region of the State had doubled, and in Galesburg, had more than quadrupled during that time. Large numbers of the students, who entered the lower classes, left before they reached the senior year of studies. While these facts were not all charged against the President, it was believed that they were in part attributable to him. His long continued hostility to some of the older members of the Board, and in particular to the founders of the College, were grave objections to him as President. Mr. Blanchard had long been aware of the feelings of the actual majority of the Board toward him and had anticipated his removal whenever there should be a full meeting. That time occurred at the Annual Meeting of the Board in June, 1857. The matter was introduced by the following resolution : "*Resolved*, That in the opinion of this Board the dissention and want of confidence, existing between President Blanchard and Professor Gale, are exerting a malign influence upon the interests of the College, and that the prosperity and efficiency of the institution require that their connection with it should be dissolved, and their places supplied by other persons : Therefore be it further *Resolved*, That President Blanchard and Professor Gale be, and they hereby are, respectfully requested to resign their places in the Faculty of Knox College." These resolutions were introduced in the morning, and were freely discussed through the whole day, President Blanchard participating in the discussion, and voting upon every question connected with the resolutions, until the final vote by which they were passed. As soon as the resolutions were passed, Mr. Blanchard and Professor Gale resigned. By this act Mr. Blanchard ceased to be a member of the Board. On the following morning, when one of the Trustees, who had voted in favor of the resolutions, was compelled to be absent from the meeting, one of the friends of Mr. Blanchard brought forward a resolution to reinstate him for one year as President of the College. This was lost, some of Mr. Blanchard's party uniting with the others in voting against it. A motion was then made and carried appointing three Trustees " a Committee of Correspondence, with a view to supply the Presidency and Professorship just made vacant." The Chairman of this Committee was taken from among the supporters of Mr. Blanchard. The Board adjourned to meet again on the second Thursday of August following, at which time they met and received the Reports of the above Committee. The majority of the Committee, who represented those members in the Board by whose united action Mr. Blanchard had been removed, presented the following Report:

" The undersigned, a majority of the Committee appointed to correspond with suitable persons to fill the vacancies occasioned by the resignation of President Blanchard and Professor Gale, hereby beg leave to report, that we have had, through one of the Committee, correspondence with several distinguished scholars of the East, any one of whom, in the estimation of the Committee, might be procured. But as a positive answer could not of course be expected, we recommend a series of names, in the order hereto appended, for the Presidency of Knox College :
Rev. Asa D. Smith.
Prof. (D. Howe) Allen, Lane Seminary.
Rev. Albert Barnes, Philadelphia.
Prof. J. B. Condit, Auburn Seminary.
Rev. M. L. R. P. Thompson, Buffalo.
And we also hereby recommend as the successor of Rev. G. W. Gale, Rev. Jno. W. Bailey.
W. E. WITHROW,
G. W. GALE."

Rev. F. Bascom, Chairman of this Committee, who is the acknowledged leader of the Congregational party in the Board, presented a minority report as follows :

" The minority of the Committee would respectfully recommend the appointment of Rev. J. Blanchard as President, and Rev. J. W. Bailey as Professor, to fill the existing vacancies. The recommendation of Mr. Bailey is based upon the expectation of Mr. Blanchard's restoration. If the Board refuse to re-elect Mr. Blanchard, then it is recommended that the vacant Professorship be filled only temporarily."

At the meeting of the Board when these resolutions were presented, one of the members, who had voted in favor of the resignation of Mr. Blanchard, was absent, confined on a sick-bed at Pepin,

Wisconsin. Another Presbyterian member, who had acquiesced in the removal of Mr. Blanchard, had been induced afterward to favor his restoration at this meeting, *merely however as a conciliatory measure*, and only *on the express condition* that Mr. Blanchard should resign again of his own accord at the close of the year. From these causes, the party who had removed Mr. Blanchard, and who believed that only embarrassment and mischief would result from his temporary restoration, and who were therefore determined if possible to appoint a new President, found themselves in an accidental minority of one, at this meeting.

The two Reports of the Committee were accepted, after which the "Board adjourned until three o'clock P. M., to hold an *informal* meeting, with a view of uniting in some definite action." The members of the Board immediately assembled in this informal meeting, and the friends of Mr. Blanchard were then asked to select, from the list of names presented in the majority report, the name of any one who would be most acceptable to them as President, in order that he might be elected by a unanimous vote. They refused to make such a selection, but expressed their full determination to reinstate Mr. Blanchard. The Faculty of the College, at that time, was composed of four Congregationalists, and only one Presbyterian. It was manifestly just, therefore, that a Presbyterian should be appointed to the Professorship made vacant by the resignation of Mr. Gale, and which had always been filled by a Presbyterian. Yet, as a measure of peace, at this meeting, the Presbyterian party proposed to yield the Professorship to the Congregationalists, *provided* they would unite in electing to the Presidency any one of the gentlemen named in the Majority Report, and provided also, they would present some unobjectionable name for the Professorship. This proposition was presented in writing by the Hon. O. H. Browning, in these words: "*Resolved*, that when we re-assemble as a Board of Trustees, we will proceed to elect Dr. A. D. Smith, of New York, or Professor Allen, of Lane Seminary, President of Knox College; and will, at the same time, proceed to elect any qualified and unobjectionable gentleman of the Congregational Church, who may be named by the Congregational members of this Board, to the Professorship of Moral Philosophy and Belles Lettres."

They were assured at the same time, that they would not be restricted to the two names contained in the resolution, but might select from the whole number presented in the majority report. *This proposition was rejected at once by the Congregationalists*, who insisted upon Mr. Blanchard as President. Before the vote was taken upon the resolution, one of their nnmber stated, that if the proposition should be accepted, he should present the name of Rev. Charles Beecher, for the vacant Professorship. To this it was replied, that it was well known that Mr. Beecher was very objectionable to a majority of the whole Board—that his name had once already been before the Board at a regular meeting, and had been rejected—that he could not be the only man in the Congregational Church, who was qualified for the Professorship—and that if they would present *only two* names for the place, one of them would, without any objection, be accepted and elected. To this offer no response was made. A motion was then made by a Congregational member, that Mr. Browning's resolution *be laid upon the table*, which was carried, by the unanimous vote of *all the supporters* of Mr. Blanchard.

Rev. F. Bascom then moved that the informal meeting be adjourned, and that they re-assemble in the regular place of meeting, and then, in accordance with the recommendation of his minority report, proceed to elect Mr. Blanchard and Mr. Bailey. This motion was carried by the united vote of those who had rejected the liberal resolution presented by Mr. Browning. Thus the informal meeting was adjourned.

There remained to the party who had removed Mr. Blanchard only this simple alternative,—either to go into the regular meeting, and thus allow the Congregationalists who were then an accidental majority, to force Mr. Blanchard upon the College again, or else to remain away from the meeting, and thereby deprive the other party of a quorum, and thus save the College from what they believed would be a great calamity. They did not hesitate to adopt the latter course, believing that their action would be justified by all good men who knew the facts in the case. The other party met, but were without a quorum. They, however, recommended to the Executive Committee of the Board, the appointment of Mr. Blanchard and Mr. Bailey to the vacancies during the coming year, and then adjourned. The Executive Committee, composed of five Trustees, made the appointments recommended; and thus Mr. Blanchard, after having been once removed and again rejected by the Board, became the acting President of the College for the next collegiate year.

Soon after this meeting of the Board in August, letters were received from Rev. A. D. Smith, D. D., in which he stated that it would not be possible for him, with his present relations and duties, to allow his name to be brought before the Board for election to the Presidency of the College.

The previous Committee of Correspondence, and other gentlemen interested in securing a suitable President, then pressed the matter upon the Rev. Dr. Thompson, of Buffalo, who was one of the gentlemen named in the report of the majority, presented at the late meeting of the Board. He was earnestly entreated not to reject the matter hastily, but to give to it a careful consideration. This he consented to do. Efforts were then made to persuade the friends of Mr. Blanchard to unite in electing Dr. Thompson. His well-known Christian courtesy and urbanity—his attainments as a scholar—and his eminence as a pulpit orator, it was thought, must commend him, even to the most violent partizan, as one eminently qualified for the Presidency. In the hope that all parties would unite in electing him, a special meeting was called by the acting President of the Board, to be held on the 15th day of October, 1857. It was well understood by the Congregationalists that the Presbyterians of the Board intended to bring forward the name of Dr. Thompson. When the day for the meeting arrived, every member of the Board was in Galesburg, and accordingly, the supporters of Mr. Blanchard were no longer in the majority, as they had been at the last meeting. *They therefore resolved to remain away from the appointed place of meeting.* The other members of the Board met at the appointed time and place, and remained in session during the whole day, which time was also spent by the Congregationalists, in a private caucus. The only reason for their refusal to come into the meeting, and unite in electing Dr. Thompson, was that he was a Presbyterian. They had, after the last meeting, despaired of electing Mr. Blanchard, and at this time, they had *no candidate* of their own to present. They were governed merely by their sectarian prejudices, which made them hostile to any man, however eminent, who did not belong to their own Congregational body.

Just before the close of the day, they sent into the meeting a notice that they would all come in, on condition that no election should then be held for President, and no other business transacted except to appoint a new committe to report the names of candidates for the Presidency at a future meeting. Although it was believed that this proposal was made for no other reason than to prevent an election at that time, and while it was certain that no more unobjectionable name than that of Dr. Thompson, could ever be presented, yet so anxious were the majority of the Board to secure a full vote for the President, whoever he might be, that they accepted the proposal.

The full Board then assembled, when " on motion of O. H. Browning, the following resolution was passed: *Resolved*, That John G. Sanborn, Esq., Rev. S. G. Wright, and Wm. E. Withrow, Esq., be appointed a committee to select and recommend to the Board a suitable man for the Presidency of Knox College, and that they report to the Board at a meeting hereafter to be called."

That next meeting was held on the 30th day of April, 1858, at which all the Trustees were present. The majority of the committee appointed at the last meeting presented a report, recommending " Rev. Harvey Curtis, D. D., of Chicago, as a suitable person to be elected to the Presidency of Knox College." A minority report was presented by Rev. S. G. Wright, a Congregationalist. "Mr. Browning moved that both reports be accepted, and that we proceed to the election of President." The Congregationalists, who constituted a party by themselves, in opposition to all other denominations and parties in the Board, then began a series of systematic efforts, by various motions, to delay, and if possible to hinder an election. They then *for the first time* professed a willingness to unite in electing Rev. A. D. Smith, D. D. But they were reminded that Dr. Smith's name had once been urged upon them, and that, too, when they were in a majority, and that they had deliberately voted to lay upon the table the proposition to elect him—and further, that they knew perfectly well, that since that time, Dr. Smith had positively refused to allow his name to be presented as a candidate for the vacant Presidency. They then proposed Rev. Dr. Thompson. But again they were reminded of the fact, that only a few months before, the Board had been called together, in a special meeting, for the express purpose of electing Dr. Thompson, and that they, in order to prevent his election, had factiously absented themselves from that meeting, until they had extorted a pledge from the other members of the Board, that they would not elect him at that time. They were reminded also that Dr. Thompson had refused, since then, to be a candidate for the office.

Becoming well satisfied, after a large portion of one day had been spent in this manner, that the Congregational members were fully resolved not to vote for any man as President who was a Presbyterian, *unless he were one who had already assured them he would not accept if elected*—and that their only object in desiring a Congregationalist as President, was that they, as Congregationalists, might control the Board and the College—and that no good could result from any longer delay, the majority of the Board proceeded to elect Rev. Harvey Curtis, D. D., as President. Every Congregationalist voted against him. All the other members of the Board, consisting of representatives of four different denominations, and of two who had no church relations, voted for him. Yet these same Congregationalists, who rejected successively, Doctors Smith, and Thompson, and Allen, and Barnes, and Condit, solely because they were Presbyterians, have not, to this day, ceased their outcry against that majority, whom they denounce before the public as "intensely sectarian!"

Let the foregoing history of the action of both parties in the Board, taken from the College records, show which party was guilty of "intense sectarianism."

The College Board is at present divided as follows: Eleven Congregationalists, ten Presbyterians, one Episcopalian, one Baptist, and two Non-professors. The College Faculty consists of seven Professors and one Tutor, of which number, three are Presbyterians and five are Congregationalists. These Congregationalists in the Faculty, have all been appointed by the unanimous votes of all the Presbyterian party in the Board, and they have the full confidence and support of that party. The question was never raised, in appointing them, to what denomination they belonged. They were appointed solely because qualified for their position. Since the removal of Mr. Blanchard, the Presbyterians in the Board have created an Assistant-Professorship, and have filled it by a Congregationalist, nominated by themselves. These facts show that the majority of the Board have no sectarian plan to accomplish. How can a party, composed of so many elements, in which four different denominations are represented, be called sectarian? The word can apply only to that party, which consists wholly of men of one denomination, and who all act in concert to gain a denominational end. There is one such party in the Board of Knox College. The end sought for is apparent. If they are not content with a larger number of Trustees than any other denomination,

FACTS ESTABLISHED.   87

and with more than one-half of the College Faculty, what would satisfy them? They profess to desire only a fair representation in the administration of the College. They have now the lion's share. To ask more for themselves than they now have, is simply to ask for all power in the College. Whether they ought to have that, let the foregoing facts determine.

The public are now in possession of the records and various documents belonging to the College, which will enable all to judge of the questions by whom it was founded and endowed, and to whom it of right belongs. They have the testimony of the men who founded the College on these very points. From the foregoing statements, the following facts among others, are fully established:

1. The Plan of the College originated with Mr. Gale.
2. The College was founded by him and the Subscribers to his Plan.
3. They did this as Subscribers to that Plan, and not in any other relation.
4. They paid, in money, to accomplish their Plan, more than the whole sum at first subscribed by them.
5. The founders of the College endowed it with property which has been worth to it already, almost five hundred and fifty thousand dollars.
6. Less than one-thirtieth of the money, which bought the land, which has so enriched the College, came from Congregationalists; all the rest came from Presbyterians.
7. The College has received *since* it was founded, donations amounting in round numbers to $46,000. Less than one-fourth of this amount was donated by Congregationalists; all the rest by Presbyterians.
8. The founders of the College, thirty-four in number, were all Presbyterians except one, who was a Congregationalist.
9. Of these founders, a large number have declared in writing that they intended to transmit the control of the College to Presbyterians.
10. In fact, the College was during many years governed almost wholly by Presbyterians, and an overwhelming majority of all its Trustees have been chosen from that denomination.
11. The present number of Congregationalists in the Board is the result in part of a change in denominational relations of some who were Presbyterians when elected Trustees. So many Congrega-

tionalists as are now in it, were never appointed, as such, by the Board.

12. Congregationalists have been divested of no rights whatever in the College, and their dissatisfaction with their present power is proof that they desire the entire supremacy.

13. The whole course of the majority of the Board in appointing a successor to Mr. Blanchard was wise, and liberal, and forbearing. They proposed the very man, Rev. A. D. Smith, D. D., whom the Congregationalists now profess to have desired as President of the College; and their proposal to elect him was laid upon the table by Congregational votes.

14. The appointments made by the Board to the College Faculty, indicate fully that no sectarian or narrow policy governs the majority. That majority is composed of men who are members or supporters of New School and Old School Presbyterian, Episcopalian, and Baptist churches. The elements of which the party is composed show that they can never be governed by any mere prejudice for a sect. They have been governed by their knowledge of what was right, in view of the fact that the College was founded and endowed by Presbyterians. They intend to be governed by that fact, hereafter, in all their action as a Board.

"RIGHTS OF CONGREGATIONALISTS IN KNOX COLLEGE."

This is the title of a Report presented at the annual meeting of the Congregational General Association of Illinois, held in Bloomington, in May last, and which was adopted *unanimously* by that body, and ordered to be printed and distributed. The Report was presented by the following seven gentlemen, who had been appointed the year before: Rev. W. W. Patton, C. G. Hammond, Esq., Hon. Owen Lovejoy, Rev. Wm. Carter, Rev. S. H. Emery, Willard Keyes, Esq., and Rev. J. Emerson. The Report was professedly occasioned by the action of the Presbytery of Peoria and Knox, at their meeting in September, 1857, when the controversy respecting Knox College was raging in its greatest violence, and when Dr. Edward Beecher, in particular, had been so far overcome by excited feeling as to forget both the courtesies and proper province of public controversy, and was using the press, East and West, and the Congregational pulpits of the principal cities in this State, in an ungenerous and wholly unprovoked onset upon the character of those members of the College Board by whom Mr. Blanchard had been removed, and f all their Presbyterian supporters. In their action, the Presbytery stated that they had "incontestable evidence of the following facts, viz: That the idea of founding Knox College originated among Presbyterians; that it was successfully carried into execution by them; that almost the whole amount of property, by means of which the College has been carried on successfully for twenty years, and which now constitutes its large endowment, was given by them; that it was, for more than ten years after its foundation, under their entire control; and that its founders desired and expected that the Presbyterian body should have a larger share in the control of the Institution than any other body."

The Presbytery also took action respecting the assaults of Rev. Dr. Beecher upon their members, which action will be given in its proper place hereafter.

To inquire whether these statements of the Presbytery were true or not, and whether their action concerning Dr. Beecher was well founded or not, was the professed object for which the above named Committee were appointed by the Association. To accomplish the object of their appointment, in learning the facts concerning the founders of Knox College, and the sources and amount of the money by which it has been endowed, would require, as every one can see, much time spent in examining the records, and Treasurer's books, and all other documentary evidence belonging to the College. These are the principal sources to which any one must apply for full and reliable information on the points to be investigated by the Committee. To examine these documents with proper care is the work, as the writer hereof knows from experience, not of hours, but of many laborious days. The important nature of the facts to be investigated demanded of the Committee the most patient and faithful examination of all the evidence to be obtained. The fact that their Report would affect materially the interests of the College concerned, and the relations of Presbyterians and Congregationalists throughout the State, made it the imperative duty of that Committee to leave no book or paper unexamined, which related to the matter committed to them. Whether that Committee were faithful to their trust, and pursued that laborious process of careful investigation which the nature of the case, and the importance of the matter demanded of them; and whether they even made any investigation whatever, shall be answered by their own published records, which are as follows:

"The Committee, by appointment of the Chairman, met Tuesday, at 10 o'clock A. M., September 28th, 1858, at the Lecture Room of the First Church of Christ, in Galesburg, Ill. Rev. Wm. W. Patton, and brother Charles G. Hammond, of Chicago—Rev. S. H. Emery, and brother Willard Keyes, of Quincy, a majority of the Committee, were present." [The minutes then give the items of the organization of the Committee, and other matters preparatory to their work, including "an order of investigation and business to be pursued in the public meeting." This consumed the morning hours, and the Committee adjourned until after dinner. The minutes then state as follows:]

"1½ o'clock P. M. The Committee met and the exercises were opened with prayer by Rev. S. H. Emery. The Chairman stated that in their investigation the Committee would pursue the order of subjects found in the action of the Presbytery of Peoria and Knox taken at its meeting in Galesburg, Sept. 10th, 1857, and published by its direction in the secular and religious papers. The messenger reported that he had delivered the note of invitation into the hands of Mr. Bailey, and that no reply was sent back.

The remainder of the afternoon was spent in listening to arguments by Rev. J. Blanchard, Ex-President of Knox College, against the positions of the Presbytery, and in examining witnesses upon the various points raised, among whom were Rev. Messrs. Blanchard, E. Beecher and L. H. Parker, and Messrs. Colton, Simmons, Tompkins, Henry Ferris and De Long.

Various printed and written documents were also placed in the hands of the Committee, among which were certified copies of the plot of the farm lands which had been sold by the College, and of the records of the county, showing to whom such lands had been deeded by the College. Adjourned till 7 o'clock P. M.

7 o'clock P. M. The session was opened with prayer by the Chairman. The meeting was held in the church to accommodate the great number in attendance, and the edifice was filled by a large and deeply interested congregation representing all parties. The investigation was resumed, and President Blanchard heard still further, and the following witnesses examined, viz.: Rev. L. H. Parker, and Dr. E. Beecher, and Messrs. H. Ferris, W. Ferris, E. Farnham and Paine. Additional printed and written documents were introduced.

The Chairman and other members of the Committee repeatedly called upon those present to bear any testimony, make any statement, or offer any suggestion relevant to any of the topics that had been brought forward.

Rev. Edward Beecher, D. D., was then heard in defense of himself against the charges made in the official paper of the Presbytery, vindicating his motives and conduct in the part which he had taken in the controversy respecting the College.

"RIGHTS OF CONGREGATIONALISTS." 91

At a late hour, after the Chairman had made a final call for further evidence or suggestions from any quarter, the Committee adjourned to meet in Chicago, at the call of the Chairman, at some time during the sessions of the Triennial Convention, to meet Oct. 20th.

Oct. 21, 1858. The Committee met in Chicago at 9 o'clock A. M., and spent an hour in an interchange of views and in hearing the first part of the Report which had been drawn up by the Chairman. Adjourned till to-morrow morning at 9 o'clock.

Oct. 22, 9 o'clock A. M. The Committee met and the session was opened with prayer by the Chairman. The consideration of the Report was resumed, which was very carefully read and considered, paragraph by paragraph, with the evidence sustaining each position. After the unanimous adoption of the Report, the Chairman was directed to prepare a copious Appendix, containing the evidence upon which the Report was based, said Appendix to be submitted to the Committee for approval at a future meeting.

April 25, 1859. The Committee met at the call of the Chairman, in Chicago, and heard the Appendix, which was approved. Adjourned till meeting of General Association, at Bloomington.

May 27, 1859. The Committee met at Bloomington, Ill., for a final consideration of the Report and Appendix, which were unanimously approved and ordered to be laid before the General Association.

Attest, } WM. W. PATTON, *Chairman.*
S. H. EMERY, *Secretary.*"

The foregoing records show the following facts:

1. That the Committee spent only *one afternoon and evening*, after they were organized, in accomplishing the great work committed to them by the General Association.

2. That the *whole afternoon,* and a part—the principal part in fact—of the evening, were "spent in listening to arguments by Rev. J. Blanchard, Ex-President of Knox College, against the positions of the Presbytery, and in examining witnesses upon the various points raised." I ask the reader if "listening to an argument by Mr. Blanchard" was an INVESTIGATION? The Committee well knew what Mr. Blanchard's feelings toward the College were. They knew what his views were on the questions in controversy, for he had published them more than a year before. The Presbytery had made a statement fully denying the truth of Mr. Blanchard's declarations. This Committee were sent to Galesburg to learn the truth of these matters, and they spent almost their whole time in listening to an argument from Mr. Blanchard. A few witnesses were examined on unimportant points—a few papers, prepared

principally by Mr. Blanchard, or under his direction, were received by them; but the records of the College—the books of the Treasurer—the valuable reports and other documents on file with the Secretary, *were not examined*, even for one moment. This Committee did not investigate at all the matters in controversy. Do the public wonder now why leading Presbyterians in Galesburg did not come before that Committee and state what facts they knew in the case? Had the Committee applied to the College Board, or its proper officers, for permission to examine the documents in their possession, and thereby indicated a determination to investigate thoroughly the whole question in controversy, then would Presbyterians have aided them gladly. But when the Committee assumed the position of a COURT, as they did, and left to Presbyterians the alternative of coming before them and *proving their own case*, or else of losing it by mere default, then it was resolved that the Committee might grope their own way, under their own chosen guides, "blind leaders of the blind."

3. The Minutes show further, that when Mr. Blanchard had ended his argument against the Presbytery, then "Rev. Edward Beecher, D. D., was heard *in defense of himself!*" In this way the Committee investigated this part of the case; as though they did not know already what Dr. Beecher thought of himself. And then—the labors of the Committee ended—they adjourned "at a late hour, *to meet* in Chicago" in three weeks from that time.

4. The Minutes show that when the Committee met again in Chicago, after the day spent in Galesburg, they spent "*an hour*" in conversation, and in hearing the first part of the Report, *which had already* "*been drawn up by the Chairman.*" The Committee made no investigation while in Galesburg, but spent their time in listening to Mr. Blanchard and Dr. Beecher. The first time they met again, their Report was already prepared, written by the Chairman, Rev. W. W. Patton. They met again the next day, when the remainder of the Report was very carefully "read and considered, paragraph by paragraph." The CHAIRMAN was then directed to prepare an Appendix, which he did, and which was read to the other members of the Committee at a future meeting. And then the work of the Committee was done.

5. It appears that the Hon. Owen Lovejoy, Rev. J. Emerson, and Rev. W. Carter, were not present at Galesburg, when the other members of the Committee met—never saw any of the documents

which must be appealed to in such a question as the one which led to their appointment—and yet that they afterward signed the Report with the others, declaring as their closing words, that their Report was a "statement of indubitable facts." How did these gentlemen know the statements of that Report to be "indubitable facts?" Did they ever see the documents—those only which would be received in a court of justice—as proof that theirs was a statement of facts?

Here, then, we see how faithful the Committee were to their trust. Their Report, instead of rising to the dignity of a candid and careful investigation, sinks down to nothing more than a labored *indorsement of Mr. Blanchard's story*. Their Report, as to its substance, was prepared for them and put into their hands by Mr. Blanchard. The Association were, doubtless, all too willing to accept a Report, whose "indubitable facts" showed, what they had never known or dreamed of before, that Knox College had been founded and endowed by Congregationalists. The Committee confided in the judgment of their Chairman, and were willing enough to sign his Report, when it was so favorable to their cause. And their Chairman, in the fervor of his zeal against Presbyterianism, was blinded to the important fact that his Report was based upon no investigation or knowledge of his own, but that the strong-willed Ex-President had been using him as a mere Amanuensis. The result exhibits itself in a Report, every one of whose essential points flatly contradicts the Records and Treasury books, and the clear intentions of all the founders of the College. It was never before the fortune of any one man to persuade so many men, wiser and better than himself, to indorse and publish, on their own authority, so much error in so small a compass. The Committee introduce a large amount of miscellaneous matter in the appendix to their Report, as proof of their statements. They no doubt believe their own Report. Their misfortune consisted in not investigating properly the questions submitted to them. They took whatever Mr. Blanchard put into their hands, and inquired no further. They were in Galesburg—their business was to go to the College and examine its documents. This, as business men, they must have known was their duty. A large part of the public suppose they did this, as a matter of course. Their own Minutes show that they did no such thing. Every person in Galesburg knows that they did no such thing. Their "investigation" was a farce, as to its character, and an imposition upon the public as to its results. Their pretended "indubitable facts" are not facts. Their Report, however, is now doing its daily work of wrong against Knox College. That Committee have a serious account yet to settle with the Church, the general public, and their own consciences, for sending forth such a Report, based on such an investigation, to injure such an Institution.

The history contained in the foregoing pages of this pamphlet, derived from the archives of the College and from the testimony of its founders, is itself a complete answer to the Report before us. Yet, that the reader may more clearly perceive the gross errors which the Committee were so unfortunate as to indorse, I propose to compare some of the most important of their statements with the documents belonging to the College. Before doing this, the attention of the reader is asked for one moment to the confidence with which the Committee assert the truth of their Report. In their closing remarks, " the Committee unanimously declare that the allegations of the Presbytery are in every respect unfounded, and are indeed so opposite to the facts as to threaten to bring great discredit upon the statements emanating from ecclesiastical bodies." The Presbytery, it will be remembered, stated that Knox College had been founded and endowed mainly by Presbyterians. The Committee submitted their Report as a "statement of indubitable facts." They declare in their minutes, that "the Report was very carefully read, and considered paragraph by paragraph, *with the evidence sustaining each position.*" Thus they plight their honor as men to the Christian public and the world, for the truth of their Report.

1. On page 23 of the Report, and in the appendix H, the Committee endeavor to show that the " original subscription," obtained by Dr. Gale, was never collected, and that those Subscribers had a very small share in founding the College. They say, " the subscription, as such, was *abandoned*, and but *a fraction of the actual endowment* was ever contributed by the original Subscribers." And again, " as a matter of fact, whatever money came from the original Subscribers forms a *very small part of the funds of the College,* while the original subscription, as such, fell through and never was collected."

Will the reader compare this bold statement of the Committee with the College records and other documents published in the first part of this pamphlet. Those records show that it was the "*Subscribers*" to Mr. Gale's Plan, who held the several meetings there reported—who appointed the Exploring and Purchasing Committees—who raised the money which bought all the land—who founded the College—and who then donated to it land, which has since then been worth to it more than half a million of dollars. These men called themselves "Subscribers to Mr. Gale's Plan," in their minutes, and they are the same men whose names are found in the original subscription book.

2. But, say the Committee, page 58, "If the original subscription *was* paid, the money has never been accounted for to the Trustees of the College. The accounts are satisfactory and square with the facts without this sum; but if this amount be added to the money obtained by loan and otherwise, there is a large deficit, for which somebody is responsible." How do the Committee know what the "accounts" are concerning this matter? Did they ever examine them or get any statement from the Treasurer showing what they were? Their statement is absolutely false. The earliest account books of the College, consisting of a "Blotter," a "Journal," and a "Ledger," contain the names of *all* the Subscribers, except the four who took no lands. They are there *credited with more* than the whole amount of their original subscription. These books show that the College received from them all its original lands. They show that these Subscribers paid for all the lands given to the College. They show that they paid several thousand dollars more than the whole original cost of the land. The accounts of the College at the beginning are based wholly upon the donations made by those Subscribers. All these facts are the opening items of the College treasury books. There they stand facing every man who opens these books. Yet this Committee were duped into the reckless statement that the accounts do not show that anything was ever paid by the Subscribers.

3. In order to prove that the original subscription was abandoned, the Committee give, to use their own language, page 59, "the names of the original Subscribers." This list of names, they say, is a "certified copy," and was obtained "through the kindness of Professor Losey." Read what Professor Losey says:

"I have never given any copy of the names contained in the subscription book to the Committee, or to any other person. I have never certified to the correctness of any copy of those names. Mr. Blanchard, at one time last year, asked to see the book, and I went with him to an office where the subscription book then was, and requested him to examine it, that he might see how false were some of the statements which he had publicly made not long before, respecting that subscription. He examined the book and wrote something at the same time. What he wrote I know not, although I supposed he was copying the names.

Dec. 1859." N. H. LOSEY.

It turns out, then, that the "certified copy" did not come from Mr. Losey. From whom did it come?

4. That list of "the names of the original Subscribers," embracing fifty-six in all, as given by the Committee,* contains *fifteen names that are not found in the list of Subscribers in the subscription book!* They are names added to those of the Subscribers, to make out the proof that the subscription fell through. The original subscription book contains, on its first page, the printed Plan of Mr. Gale. This is immediately followed by the following heading: "We, the Subscribers, agree to pay the sums set opposite to our names respectively, to such person or persons as shall be designated by the Subscribers or Board of Trustees elected by them, for the purposes, and in the manner set forth in the foregoing printed Preamble and Plan for establishing literary institutions in the West." This is followed by the names of the Subscribers, all in *their own* handwriting, except in two or three cases, when they were written by some one else, which fact is always denoted with the initials of the person who wrote them. These names follow each other in the subscription book in close order. They are then followed by *fourteen blank pages* of the book, after which we come to a private memorandum, made by Mr. Gale while acting as agent of the Association. This memorandum is in *pencil mark*—all of it in the handwriting of Mr. Gale, and is thus headed: "Families who will go as soon (as) they can sell." After this follow fifteen names, more than half of them without any Christian name or initials prefixed. Now these fifteen names under this heading, "families who will go," etc., and separated from the Subscribers by fourteen blank pages, are all reported by the Committee as original Subscribers. Moreover, they had a "certified copy" that the list they give is correct. If any man certified to the correctness of such a list, from an examination of the subscription book, he was guilty of something worse than a mistake.

5. As further proof that the subscription fell through, the Committee say, page 59, "that but *ten* persons" of the original Subscribers "actually engaged in the enterprise and made any pay-

---

* The Subscription Book contains only forty-six names as Subscribers.

ments;" that "more than three-quarters of the original Association purchased no farms, and their subscriptions were never paid." The Day-book, and Journal, and Ledger of the College, are all before me as I write, and I see on their pages the names, not of ten only, but of thirty of these Subscribers, charged with lands bought of the Association, in January, 1836, according to the Plan. These thirty names embrace all but *four* of the Subscribers who founded the College. These Subscribers are charged with their lands as *bona fide* purchasers, and only eight of them ever returned their lands, which were only a small fraction of all that had been bought; and this most of them did, at the earnest solicitation of the agent of the College, and solely for its benefit, and not because they were unwilling to pay for them. Had the Committee taken the trouble, while in Galesburg, to step into the office of the Treasurer and examine his books, they might have learned all these facts, and thus have saved themselves from an imposition, and have spared the College and its founders the great wrong their Report has done them.

6. The Committee next endeavor to show that the sale of farm-lands to the Subscribers in Whitesboro', N. Y., in January, 1836, was only a "professed sale"—a "sale only in name"—and "the memorandum of it is entirely unreliable as showing actual, pecuniary transactions." Most unfortunate Committee! The "memorandum" of that sale, which they think is so "entirely unreliable," chances to be, first, the College records; second, a list of the lands sold and the names of the purchasers, made by the Secretary of the meeting at which the sale took place, and now on file among the papers of the College; third, the Day-book; fourth, the Journal; fifth, the Ledger of the College treasury. The whole matter stands on the opening pages of these books, and it stands there just as it has been given in the early pages of this pamphlet. The College opens its books—commences its accounts—by recording the sale made at that meeting, in the State of New York. That sale was a part of the original Plan, and until then, the College, which had just been founded, had received no endowment.

And here I pause and ask what do this Committee mean by such frequent and positive assertions concerning matters which they know nothing about, and which are contradicted in the plainest manner by the records and account books of the College? Not only has the College been injured by such unpardonable errors of statement, but the public have been grossly imposed upon, and that

7

too, by men from whom they had a right to expect a clear understanding of the things which they declare to be "indubitable facts."

7. The Committee, having shown in their Report, that the "Subscribers, as such," neither founded nor endowed the College, next endeavor to enlighten us upon the question, who were its founders and endowers? The reader will remember what the College records have said on this point. According to them the College was founded by the Subscribers, at their meeting in January, 1836, in Whitesboro', N. Y., who then appointed its Board of Trustees. It was also endowed at that meeting by the same "Subscribers" who donated to it lands from which almost all its wealth has been derived.

Now this Committee are not men who are ignorant of what is meant by founding and endowing a College. They know that the act of the Subscribers, in New York, was in every sense—in the fullest legal, technical, and moral sense—an act of founding and endowing. Then, and then only, was any action ever taken, by any one, to found Knox College. And the history of the College begins, in its own records, from that day. It was at that time also, as its own books show, that its lands, which have made it so rich, were given to it, and given for the express purpose of sustaining it in accomplishing the ends of a College. The men who originate the Plan for a College—who organize it—who appoint its Board of Trustees—and who then enrich it by their donations, are its founders and endowers. No men know this better than this Committee. Yet see how they represent this matter! They gravely tell us that the men who came as early "settlers" into Galesburg, (a place that had no existence until after the College was founded)—who never donated one dollar in money or one acre of land to the College—who bought lands, not *for* the College, but *from* it, for their own private interest—these are the men by whom Knox College was founded and endowed. The men who came to Galesburg "and purchased the original lands" then owned and offered for sale by the College, "with scholarships attached, at a high rate," did it, say the Committee, p. 24, "for the express purpose of FOUNDING *the College*." Again they say, on page 77, "there is no doubt that the original *endowment* of the College was *by the sale of the farm-lands* to those *settlers* who came during the early years of the enterprise and who chose to pay five dollars there *in order to* ENDOW *the College*, instead of purchasing at a less price elsewhere." Here we have the views of this Committee, and these views run through the whole of their Report. The men who found and endow a College are not those who originate the plan—who organize the institution —who appoint a Board of Trust—who secure for it a Charter, naming in that Charter the corporators—and who donate to it lands out of which it may realize an annual income equal to all its wants; but they are those "who came as settlers during the early years of the enterprise," who buy for their own private speculation the farm-lands which the College offers for sale to any man who is willing to pay its price. Honorable, magnanimous, "non-sectarian" Committee! In order to drag in some names that belonged to Congregationalists, and hinge upon them a claim to the College, they put aside the "Subscribers" and ignore all their acts as founders, and then represent the College as having been founded and endowed by the men who bought its farm-lands—a representation which is as absurd as it is false. Never was there a more ungenerous attempt, for mere party purposes, to falsify history, and deprive noble men of the honors due them, than this of the Committee, in endeavoring to transfer the credit of having founded and liberally endowed Knox College, from the "Subscribers" to the mixed multitude, with various interests, who constituted the early settlers of Galesburg.

8. I come now to the most important part of the Report—that upon which the Committee base almost wholly the claim of Congregationalists to Knox College. On page 29 of their Report, the Committee show that the College has received from Presbyterians, in donations and for lands sold them, only about $8,000, while it has received from Congregationalists, more than $67,000. "It thus appears," say they, "that where New School Presbyterians have contributed *one* dollar to the support and endowment of Knox College, Congregationalists have contributed *eight* dollars!" "If, then, a denominational claim is to rest upon a pecuniary basis, it is evident that the Institution should be in the hands of Congregationalists." In respect to "pure donations" made to the College, the matter stands thus in the Report: "Congregationalists have furnished *forty-nine* dollars to *one* of the real donations!" This Committee seem never to have known that the whole amount of lands which the College owned at first, was a "pure donation" from the founders. Or, if they knew it, they are careful that their readers shall never know it. The above "facts" of the Report are based

mainly upon that part of the "Appendix" embraced under the letter R., pp. 77–79. They there give a "certified list of the purchasers of the farm-lands of Knox College." They there show that Congregationalists have paid for farm-lands, above $25,000, while Presbyterians have paid for farm-lands only about $7,000. On page 25 they say, "to this part of the Appendix the Committee would call the patient attention of every reader." The list of names which they there give, is declared by them to be " drawn from the County Records." The list was also " certified to be correct by Thomas N. Ayres & Son, Real Estate Agents." Then the list was " examined by six of the early settlers, men of standing in Galesburg," who certify that the list of names, the amount purchased, and the price per acre paid by each purchaser, and also their Church relations, are all correctly stated. These six gentlemen, who vouch for the truth of the Committee's statement, are Messrs. Eli Farnham, Henry Ferris, C. S. Colton, R. Payne, L. Sanderson, and Matthew Chambers. Four of them are Congregational members of the Board of Knox College. A portion of the Report so important as this is, in its bearings upon the argument of the Committee, and so well supported by vouchers, and " County Abstracts," deserves the " patient attention " which the Committee invite to it. The reader is asked to examine it with me, in the light of the College Treasury books, and of the County Recorder's certificate, and of other undeniable facts, that it may be seen how utterly blind this Committee were, and into what depths of error they were led by the " argument" to which they listened too credulously in Galesburg.

(1.) The list furnished by the Committee contains the names of those who " purchased the farm-lands of Knox College," and because they did this they are claimed as the actual " founders " and " endowers " of the College. To this point it is enough to say, that if the list were perfectly correct, it would have nothing to do with the question before the Committee. It requires no great amount of sense to know that the College must have been *founded* before it could own lands to sell to " early settlers," or to any one else. The real question is, who were those founders ? Certainly they were not those who bought lands from the College. Then, it requires no more sense to know that the men who bought these lands *from* the College, did not, in so doing, *endow it*. The men who *gave those lands* to the College were the men by whom it was *endowed*. Does the reader suppose our Committee were so ignorant as not to know these things? And if they did know them, what are we to think of their attempt to mislead the public on these points? They have committed a great fault. It must be charged either against the *head* or against the *heart*. The Committee may choose for themselves which it shall be. If the Committee honestly believed that the purchasers of lands from the College, and not those who donated the lands to the College, are its "founders and endowers," why were they not consistent with themselves in their Report? They state that Judge Phelps gave to the College eighteen quarter-sections of *land*, and therefore *he* is credited with almost the whole present endowment of the College. But, according to their previous representations, Judge Phelps did nothing toward endowing the College with his lands: The men who *bought* those lands from the College are the men to whom that credit belongs. Is not this something worse than nonsense? But again, if the men who bought College lands for themselves, are its only real benefactors, then why have the Committee inquired only concerning the purchasers of *farm-lands?* The village property has been worth far more than the farm-lands of the College.

The College has at interest, at the present time, above $200,000. It has expended for buildings more than $100,000. It has expended in other ways above $200,000. The College lands have thus furnished it with money, or its equivalent, to an amount exceeding half a million of dollars. The Committee have endeavored to show us the sources whence only $43,000 of this amount have been derived. But if the men who furnished $43,000, by buying College lands, are to be regarded as its endowers, are not those who furnished more than $450,000, in exactly the same way, to be regarded also as having done something toward its endowment? It seems puerile to labor to meet such positions as the above, and yet they are the essential points in the Report of the Committee.

(2.) The list furnished by the Committee contains fifty-nine names of persons, all of whom are represented as having been among the "early settlers" of Galesburg, and who bought "during the early years of the enterprise." "They paid the money *which started* the College." "They were the men who bought of the *Association*," and *none of them* are included among those who came in at a later day and "bought of the *College, since* it has been endowed." How much truth there is in this part of the Report, will appear from the following facts, *taken from the College books*, concerning some of the names in the list of the Committee:

W. A. Wood, purchased in 1854, 19 years after College was founded.
S. Richardson,   "   "   "   "   "   "
A. B. Clark,   "   "   "   "   "   "
G. W. G. Ferris, "   "   "   "   "   "
L. Gary,   "   "   "   "   "   "
J. Jerauld,   "   1846, 11   "   "   "
A. G. Pearson,   "   1853, 18   "   "   "
W. D. Lee,   "   1850, 15   "   "   "
J. Blanchard,   "   1852, 17   "   "   "

The above facts show that the Committee knew nothing about the matter of which they wrote.

A large number of those reported in their list as having purchased at "an early date," purchased only within the last few years. And their list embraces some who never purchased any farm-lands of the College at any time.

(3.) Every one of the fifty-nine purchasers is reported as having paid exactly *five dollars* an acre for his land. "They bought at five dollars an acre:" "They chose to pay five dollars instead of purchasing at a less price elsewhere." Now the simple fact is, that hardly one of all the actual purchasers in that list bought at exactly five dollars an acre. Every one of the six men, who vouch for the correctness of the list, paid on an average more than that price for the land they bought. To see how remote from the truth this Committee are, look at the following names as they stand on the College books:

L. Gary,   paid per acre, $25
A. G. Pearson,   "   "   "   30
W. A. Wood,   "   "   "   25
S. Richardson,   "   "   "   22
A. B. Clark,   "   "   "   21
G. W. G. Ferris,   "   "   "   30
J. Blanchard,   "   "   "   15

The number of names might be increased with a like result as this until it embraced *full three-fourths* of all reported by the Committee who were actual purchasers of the College lands. But my only object is to present enough to convince the Committee of the grave errors into which they fell.

(4.) As the price per acre, according to the Committee, was exactly five dollars, while according to the College treasury it was in almost every case much more than that, so the amounts paid by each one, as given by the Committee, are, in most cases, much less than those credited on the Treasurer's books:

W. A. Wood,	paid as per Report,	$600	as per Treasurer,	$3,850
S. Ferris,	" " " "	1,200	" " "	3,160
G. W. Gale,	" " " "	1,200	" " "	3,980
G. W. G. Ferris,	" " " "	1,500	" " "	8,630
N. West,	" " " "	600	" " "	1,480
A. G. Pearson,	" " " "	400	" " "	2,400
L. Gary,	" " " "	400	" " "	2,000
J. Blanchard,	" " " "	800	" " "	2,400

The reader can see how much credit is to be given to the claims of the Committee in behalf of Congregationalists when they are founded upon such statements as theirs above. The Committee find that all the Presbyterian purchasers together paid only about $7,000. In the above list the first five names are those of Presbyterians, who, it will be seen, paid more than $21,000. One of those Presbyterians alone paid more than the Committee have credited to that whole class in their entire list.

(5.) According to the Committee only nine of all the fifty-nine names in their list were Presbyterians, and they only purchased to the aggregate amount of $7,400. Now if these nine were all the purchasers who were Presbyterians, which they are not, still the treasury books show that these same nine bought farm-lands to the amount of $16,910.

(6.) The Committee profess to give only the names of purchasers at an early day. In classifying them as Congregationalists or Presbyterians they credit to the former class all *who now* "*sustain* the two Congregational Churches in Galesburg." This is certainly an easy method of settling a question about matters that occurred, as they claim, twenty and more years ago. Many of those "who now sustain the two Congregational Churches" in this place, were Presbyterians twenty years ago, and never then had even a dream that they would ever become Congregationalists. Some of them are yet Presbyterians. As proof of these points read the following certificate from one of those reported as Congregational purchasers:

"I hereby certify that I was a Presbyterian when I bought my land of the Agent of the College, and have never changed my sentiments.

HENRY WILCOX.

GALESBURG, July 28, 1859."

This gentleman "supports one of the Congregational Churches in Galesburg." What he declares to be true of himself is true of not a few of those claimed by the Committee as Congregationalists.

(7.) In the list of the Committee are a number of names, as purchasers from the College, who in fact did not buy of the College, but of some other party. As proof of this point read the following statement from one of the "supporters of one of the Congregational Churches" in this place:

"I hereby certify that I had been for many years previous to coming here, an officer in a Presbyterian Church, and that I united with the Church in this place as a Presbyterian. The land which I purchased had *passed through several hands* after it was sold by the College before I came in possession of it. I assumed a part of the indebtedness to the Trustees, and as was customary in such cases, I received my deed from them.

JOEL MARTIN.

GALESBURG, Aug. 1859."

(8.) The Committee throw out of the account seven names embraced in their list because their "sentiments are not known." At first view this seems very fair, but when it proves to be a fact, well known to others if not to the Committee, that all of these seven were Presbyterians, except one, who was *not* a Congregationalist, then the ignorance of the Committee assumes a suspicious hue. Their ignorance occurred at that fortunate moment when it would have been "folly to be wise." They thereby deduct several thousand dollars from the Presbyterian column.

(9.) The Committee, in this list, have been compelled to give the names of some of the "Subscribers" *as purchasers*, who are said in their Appendix "H," *not to have purchased* of the College. But that a careful reader may not discover the discrepancy, the list now under examination gives some of those names without any initials or Christian name prefixed, and others with the initials changed from those of the real purchaser. Did the Committee know this when they published that list of names?

(10.) The Committee show that Congregationalists paid at "an early day" for "farm-lands" above $25,000. The treasury books show that from the day the College was founded, in 1836, *until now*, Congregationalists have paid for farm-lands only $14,520.

(11.) According to the Committee there were *fifty-nine* who purchased at an "early day" to "start the College," only *ten* of whom were "original Subscribers," as appears in Appendix "H."

The College treasury shows that *thirty* of the original Subscribers became purchasers of farm-lands, and then that the *whole number* of purchasers, including these thirty, during the first *fourteen years* of the College was *not as great* as that given by this Committee.

(12.) But, say the Committee, "this list has been examined by six of the early settlers, men of standing in Galesburg," and they "certify that the same is, according to their best knowledge and belief, correct." Let me inform the Committee of what some of these same gentlemen say about that list. They indignantly *deny* having ever certified to the list *as it is published* in the Report. They were asked to give a list of the names of the purchasers of the College farm-lands without reference to the time of the purchase or the price to be paid. This they did as well as they were able without any documents, and trusting to their memory, which had to extend over a period of more than twenty years. And to such a list they appended their certificate. That list was changed in several important respects after it left their hands. This is what some of these gentlemen declare, and this statement is published by permission from one of them. No effort has been made to learn the views of the others, but my knowledge of those gentlemen leads me to believe that none of them certified to the correctness of the list in the form published by the Committee. They knew that list to be incorrect. And here let me ask this Committee why they went to these gentlemen to learn who had bought College lands at an early day ? Did they not know that the College books were the proper sources of information on that point ? Did not such a gentleman as C. G. Hammond, Esq., who manages one of the largest and most complicated business interests of this country, know that it was sheer folly to go about the streets of Galesburg asking for information as to who bought the College lands, when the College Treasurer was in possession of every fact, and *as a Congregationalist* would cheerfully have given any information needed ? The truth is, the Committee simply published what had already been prepared for them by another party—and the man who prepared the materials of that Report *dared not go to the College books for facts.* All Galesburg guesses who that man is.

(13.) Not only did six gentlemen certify to the correctness of the list, but, say the Committee, it was "drawn from the county records," it is a "certified abstract from the county records, pp. 77, 24." If this were so, it would not show that the persons there named actually bought of the College and "paid the money" to the College. Many persons here have deeds from the College, who never paid to its treasury a dollar. This has already been explained. But now mark what follows: A few names were selected from the Committee's list, enough to test the point involved, and were given to the County Recorder, who was directed to certify under the seal of his office whether they are found upon the county records as purchasers of farm lands from the College *at any time*, whether at an "early" date or at any date. This is his certificate:

"STATE OF ILLINOIS, } ss.
   Knox County, } I, Cephas Arms, Clerk of the Circuit Court, and *Ex-Officio* Recorder in and for said Knox county, do hereby certify that the names of Jones Harding, W. E. Holyoke, Hugh Conger, Sherman Williams, William Lee, —— Dutton, S. Richardson and W. A. Wood, are not found upon the Records of Knox county, as purchasers of farm-lands from the Trustees of Knox M. L. College.

In witness thereof, I have hereunto affixed my name and the seal of said office, at Knoxville, this 9th day of August, A. D., 1859.

                    CEPHAS ARMS, *Clerk*. [SEAL.]"

Now, as a matter of fact, some of the parties named by the Recorder did buy lands of the College, and paid the money for them; but before their payments were completed, they sold to some one else, and *that* person to whom they sold received the deed, and his name is the one that will be found on the county records. Our Committee, however, assert that the foregoing names are taken from the county records. The certificate of the Recorder shows that they are *not* upon those records, as purchasers from the College.

(14.) But once more, say this sagacious Committee, the list is not only taken from the county records, and vouched for as correct, by "six gentlemen of standing in Galesburg," but it is also "certified to be correct by Thomas N. Ayres & Son, Real Estate Agents." Read now what Thomas N. Ayres & Son say on that point:

                    "GALESBURG, Jan. 17th, 1860.

We do hereby certify, that the statement of the 'purchasers of farm-lands from Knox College,' purporting to have been certified to by Thomas N. Ayres & Son, Real Estate Agents, in 'Appendix R.,' to 'a Report of the Committee of Investigation of the General Association of Illinois,' entitled 'Rights of Congregationalists in Knox College,' *is materially different* from the statement furnished by us, heretofore, to Rev. J. Blanchard.

                                 AYRES, BATES & CO.,
                              Successors of Thos. N. Ayres & Son."

These gentlemen were not willing to risk their reputation for business accuracy, by allowing the statement of the Committee concerning them to go uncorrected. The secret is all out, too, through their certificate, as to who furnished the Committee with their extraordinary list of names! That list is incorrect in every essential respect. Yet upon that list of names is built up almost the whole argument in behalf of the "Rights of Congregationalists in Knox College." In leaving this part of the Report, I must say that I know not whether to wonder most at the audacity of the man who ventured to impose that statement upon such men as composed this Committee, or at the unaccountable credulity of the Committee in receiving it. No "camel" appears to have been too great for their receptive powers, provided it favored their cause. They proved every statement, they say, "paragraph by paragraph," and yet they reported, in their list of names, that of Mr. Blanchard, as one who bought of the College, at an early day, at five dollars an acre, to the amount of $800, which he paid, to "start the College." Yet Mr. Blanchard did not come to Galesburg until ten years after the College had been founded, and he did not buy any of its lands until almost seven years after he came here, and he was to pay for them $2,400, at $15 an acre, and the College indorsed upon his unpaid note, as a donation, two-thirds of the whole sum, *since* his removal from its Presidency. Truly the Committee have stated "indubitable facts!"

9. I have already called the reader's attention to a statement of the Committee, respecting the value of the donation made to the College by Hon. Charles Phelps. They say, p. 26, that donation was "estimated to be worth at the time $30,000," and it now constitutes "the principal part of the College endowment of over $300,000!" I have shown that the donation was not estimated to be worth $15,000 when made, and that it is not yet worth $30,000. How could the Committee have made such a mistake?

But I have a special object in recalling this matter at this time. When the Report of the Committee was adopted by the unanimous vote of the General Association, there were present, as members of the Association, according to its Minutes, the following Trustees of the College: Rev. F. Bascom, Rev. W. E. Holyoke, Rev. S. G. Wright, Rev. H. Foote, and E. Farnham, Esq. Now these five gentlemen have been in attendance upon all the meetings of the Board of the College, from the time the donation of Mr. Phelps was made, to the present. They were present when that donation was made. The College records show this to be true. They heard the report of the Treasurer the next year, 1854, when he gave the value of that donation at $20,356.95. They accepted his report, at that time, as true. They have heard his annual reports from that time until the present year. Some of them have served on a Committee to determine the manner of using the money received from the sale of those lands. I ask these gentlemen how, as ministers of the Gospel, and Christian men, they could vote for the Report of the Committee, when *they knew* that part of it relating to the Phelps donation to be so untrue? How can they justify themselves to the Commitee, saying nothing of the public, for allowing them to fall into so immense an error? Are we to think that they are willing to allow any statement, however untrue, to go forth to the public, that will damage Knox College, and the interests of Presbyterianism? But let us view the matter from another stand-point. In less than *four weeks* after these Trustees had voted for the Report of the Committee in the Association, and directed it to be " printed and distributed," they met in Galesburg, in the annual meeting of the College Board. At that meeting, the Treasurer presented his annual report, in which he gave, *as an item by itself*, the present value of the Phelps donation at $26,272.15.

This report was accepted without a word of objection. Yet according to the Report of the Committee, for which these five Trustees had only a few days before voted, the Treasurer made the enormous mistake of at least $300,000, in his estimate of the value of the Phelps' donation. Did these Trustees charge him with this mistake? Did they object to the Report on that account? Did they, as honest guardians of a great trust, inquire at all, what had become of the "munificent bequest of the late Hon. Charles Phelps, now constituting the principal part of the College endowment, of over $300,000 "? Not a word of the kind was heard from one of them. Yet the published Report of the Committee, containing these errors, was very busily circulated during that meeting of the Board, and at the Commencement exercises of the College.

10. On page 51 of the Report is a certificate, signed by Mr. Blanchard and seven Congregational Trustees of the College, that in 1854 a "compromise resolution" was adopted by the united votes of the whole Board, "binding the Board, in all future elections, to abstain from any party action." But, say they, when the party

opposed to Mr. Blanchard "obtained an accidental majority they denied the force of the said resolution, and did not hesitate to violate it *by the election* of men to the Board *by a strictly party vote*."
Now, since 1854 there have been but two Trustees elected to the Board, viz.: C. M. Pomroy and Thomas G. Frost. On examining the College records, I find the following minutes respecting these elections: "Voted, that the place of Peter Butler (a Baptist,) in this Board, be declared vacant." "Several names were proposed, and voted upon, without effecting an election, when a recess of fifteen minutes was taken for *consultation*." "After the expiration of the time above named, the members again took their seats, when Mr. Browning nominated Caleb M. Pomroy, of Quincy, (a Baptist,) who was then *unanimously* elected a Trustee of Knox College." This was in 1856. In 1858, Mr. S. Ferris resigned his place as a Trustee. His place, according to the records, was filled as follows: "Thomas G. Frost was then nominated and *unanimously* elected a Trustee of Knox College." So much for the violation of a compromise "by the election of *men* to the Board by a *strictly* party vote." The only two men elected, have been elected by the votes of the whole Board.

The same Trustees, who gave the above certificate, have also, on pp. 51, 52, certified that the party opposed to Mr. Blanchard, did, in 1849, leave a meeting of the Board, in order to deprive it of a quorum—and that in 1857 they absented themselves from another meeting, for the same purpose. They certify, also, that "we (the Congregationalists) proposed to them (the rest of the Board) that we would vote for a non-sectarian President, such as Rev. Asa D. Smith, D. D., which proposition they refused to accept." Dear reader, did you ever think why Paul joined together those two asseverations, "I speak the truth *and* lie not"?

As a commentary thereon, notice these facts: The meetings in 1849 and in 1857, *were* broken up in the manner certified. But from the *honest* indignation which these gentlemen, who sign the certificate, express for such acts, do you not understand them to claim entire exemption from all acts of the same kind? Yet, in October, 1857, they absented themselves a whole day from a meeting of the Board, solely in order to *prevent the election* of Rev. Dr. Thompson, of Buffalo, as President of the College.

It is true, also, that they *did* offer to elect Rev. A. D. Smith, D.D.; but that was in 1858, when Dr. Curtis' name was before them for election, and when *they knew* that Dr. Smith had, long before, positively refused to be a candidate for the Presidency, and when *they* had, the year before, being then a majority, *voted to lay on the table* the motion to elect Dr. Smith!

11. The Congregational Trustees complain that the other parties in the Board have violated a "compromise resolution," which, they claim, bound "the Board, in all future elections, to abstain from any party action." No compromise resolution having such a sense as they put upon it, has ever been passed by the Board. But if such a resolution had been passed, I leave the reader to judge for himself which party has violated it, by "party action," after recalling the fact that the Congregationalists have been a party, by themselves, in the Board, during all the attempts of the Board to fill the vacancies occasioned by the resignation of Mr. Blanchard and Mr. Gale. They rejected Doctors Smith, and Allen, and Condit, and Barnes, and Thompson, and voted against Dr. Curtis on no other ground than that they were Presbyterians. They were the only party who were composed of men of one denomination, and no more. And yet, with amazing blindness, they charge "party action" and "intense sectarianism," upon all the other members of the Board, who represent four different denominations.

12. The Committee are equally determined to prove that the majority of the Board are wretchedly "sectarian," although it numbers, among its members, a Baptist, an Episcopalian, and both Old and New School Presbyterians. They, however, very conveniently style them all New School Presbyterians, and then, by a sort of Aristotelian process, prove them to be sectarian, because, as they assert, the whole denomination is so. In this line of argument they refer to the recent "unanimous votes in the General Assembly, on the subjects of Church Extension, Church Erection, Home and Foreign Missions, the Publication of books and tracts, and Ministerial Education." This "sectarian spirit," the Committee say, "has led to the establishment of sectarian Presbyterian Colleges, in this and contiguous States," and to a determination "to institute a Theological Seminary for themselves alone." Saying nothing of the logic or the truthfulness of this part of the Report, one must suppose, from the pious horror with which they announce the above misdeeds of the New School Presbyterian Church, that the Committee have never heard of any exclusively Congregational plans for Church Erection or Church Extension, or Publication, and the like. They

have, doubtless, never heard of the "Illinois Home Missionary Association," whose Corresponding Secretary is Rev. W. W. Patton, which last fact is sufficient proof that it is a Congregational Society. They never have heard of the Congregational "American Missionary Association" for Foreign Missions. They never have heard of "Church Erection Funds" contributed by their own denomination, and solely for their own use. They are no doubt totally ignorant of the existence of the "Congregational Board of Publication." They are not aware of any exclusively Congregational Colleges, in Iowa, and in other parts of the West, saying nothing of a *few Institutions*, belonging to their denomination, in that remote region of our land, which the Committee may have heard about, by the name of New England. And this Committee, certainly, are not yet informed of the fact, that Congregationalists *have* instituted " a Theological Seminary *for themselves alone*," in the city of Chicago, and that its library has pledged for its benefit all "*the net profits!*" of that preeminently non-sectarian paper, the *Congregational Herald*, whose principal editor is the Chairman of our Committee! I hope this Committee may become informed of these facts before they expend any more indignation about the "sectarianism" of the New School Presbyterian Church. As containing a full reply to all this mere verbiage of the Committee about sectarianism, I commend to them these words of an inspired Apostle: "Wherein thou judgest another, thou condemnest thyself, for thou that judgest *doest the same things.*"

Before dismissing this matter I must ask the reader's attention to the following facts: Congregationalists have the President, nearly all the Faculty, and at least an equal number, if not a majority of the Trustees of Beloit College. They have the President and their full share of the Faculty and Trustees of Illinois College. They have a majority of the Faculty, and a larger number of Trustees than New School Presbyterians have, in Knox College, Yet, solely because they cannot have the *entire* control of Knox College, they wage a furious war upon it. They have entertained, in their Association, proposals from the Wesleyan Methodists, to receive as their own, and build up the Wheaton Institute; and Mr. Blanchard has, through their agency, been appointed its President, and has already entered upon the duties of his office. This Wheaton Institute is twenty-five miles west of Chicago—has no endowment—and but little more than twenty thousand dollars' worth of property of all kinds. It is in the center of a region which embraces the Baptist University—the Methodist Institutions at Evanston—Lind University—and Beloit, and Knox, and Illinois Colleges. A College at Wheaton is not demanded by any public interests whatever—it can be sustained and endowed only by extraordinary efforts—and if it should ever be successful it must be at the expense of at least some one of the Colleges that so closely encircle it, in which Congregationalists are already interested. No reason whatever exists for building up that Institution, except that it will enable these "co-operative" Congregationalists, who have such a large share in the control of so many other Colleges, to call one College exclusively their own. If they think it wise to do this, no one objects. But for the sake of common sense as well as of honesty, while they are doing this, let them give up this whining cant about "sectarianism."

13. Having proved that the whole New School General Assembly is sectarian, and that therefore the majority of the Trustees of Knox College are so, the Committee next proceed to establish the same conclusion, by reporting what the Rev. Mr. Spencer, and the Rev. Dr. Patterson, of Chicago, have said about the College, although neither of these gentlemen have anything to do with its control. In the Appendix to the Report, letter "G," is this statement:

"Rev. L. H. Parker, of Galesburg, testified before the Committee as follows: 'Last spring I was at Geneseo, in my capacity as Trustee of the Academy in that place. There were propositions under consideration, with reference to its coming under the distinctive control of N. S. Presbyterians. I met there Rev. Mr. Spencer—N. S. Presbyterian minister, now resident in Chicago—who said that it was now the design and settled policy of his denomination to bring all the schools, academies and colleges, *in which they were interested*, under their distinctive *ecclesiastical* control. In *accomplishing* this, Knox College, he remarked, had given them more trouble than any other institution.'"

Truly, "ambition" is not the only thing that "o'erleaps itself." I suppose every reader, unless it be the Rev. L. H. Parker, knows exactly what is meant by "distinctive ecclesiastical control." A College would be under "ecclesiastical control" when controlled directly by a religious denomination, or by Trustees elected by a religious denomination. The Congregational Theological Seminary of Chicago is an instance of such control. But Knox College is, by its Charter, *a close corporation*, a self-perpetuating body, which appoints within itself all its Trustees, and therefore cannot possibly be under "ecclesiastical control." Mr. Parker knew this well enough. But in his anxiety to prove something against the College, he has proved too much. Mr. Spencer could hardly have talked about the actual "accomplishment" of the purpose of Presbyterians to bring Knox College under "distinctive *ecclesiastical* control." The thing is simply impossible, even if there were such a desire. Mr. Parker will do well to refresh his "*ecclesiastical*" knowledge, before he gives another certificate about "*ecclesiastical* control." But alas! for the Committee, Mr. Spencer denies having said what Mr. Parker has attributed to him. In a letter written to me on this subject, during the past summer, Mr. Spencer says:

"I am constrained to contradict the very explicit testimony of the Rev. L. H. Parker. I did not say that it was now the design and settled policy of my denomination to *bring* all the schools, and academies, and colleges, in which we are interested, under our ecclesiastical control. I knew that such a statement would be false. The subject of *bringing* existing co-operative institutions under *ecclesiastical* control was not mentioned. I *was opposed* to entering into any co-operative arrangement to sustain Geneseo Academy, and gave it as my opinion that such efforts would in future be discountenanced. The only reference to Knox College made by me, was to discourage the idea that a similar *union* of denominations might sustain Geneseo Academy. A frank opposition to a union effort in the case of that Academy, based upon a somewhat troublesome co-operative experience in Knox College, was a very natural occurrence. The difficulties in Knox College were referred to merely as a warning against future efforts of that kind. It is of no importance, whatever, to correct Mr. Parker's misapprehension of my personal views on this subject. But as one of three men chosen to prove the existence of a 'settled' denominational 'policy,' concerning all schools, academies and colleges, in which New School Presbyterians are interested, it is important for me to deny that I ever said there is such a policy as Mr. Parker speaks of, or that this was the cause of the troubles at Knox College. W. H. SPENCER."

Fearing that Mr. Parker might not be a witness of sufficient "standing," the Committee next introduce Rev. Edward Beecher, D. D., who is made to testify as follows:

"Before the election of Dr. Curtis to the Presidency, I had an interview with Rev. Dr. Patterson of Chicago, to see whether some investigation of facts, or reference to arbitrators, or basis of adjustment, could not be secured prior to any election by the Board of Trust. But such an effort at an accommodation of differences was wholly objected to and refused, both by Dr. P. and by Dr. Gale. Dr. P. asserted that the College belonged to the N. S. Presbyterians, and that they ought to have the entire control of it."

8

Now if the above statement were in all particulars correct, yet it may well be asked what Dr. Beecher had to do with these affairs of Knox College? He had no connection with the College whatever. He was not one of its Trustees. He was not commissioned by its Board to intercede with Dr. Patterson or any one else in their behalf. The Board were about to elect a President. Dr. Beecher attempted to prevent it. Why? Solely because they were about to elect a Presbyterian. As long as there was any hope of securing a Congregationalist as President, Dr. Beecher never thought any "investigation of facts" necessary. His proposal now was merely an attempt to delay present action by the Board, and thus, of course, get rid of Dr. Curtis as a candidate, as had been done with other candidates. But again, why appeal to Dr. Patterson? He had nothing to do with the control of the College. All who know him know that he would not dictate to the Board of Trustees what their action should be, even with the example of Dr. Beecher to encourage him. Dr. Patterson does know, if Dr. Beecher does not, what the rights of a Board of Trustees like that of Knox College are, and he would be the last man to attempt to control such a Board by *outside pressure*. Let us hear, however, what Dr. Patterson says concerning the truth of Dr. Beecher's statement.

"PROF. J. W. BAILEY:

Dear Bro.—In the pamphlet entitled 'Rights of Congregationalists in Knox College,' p. 56, I find a statement from Dr. Edward Beecher, in which a report is given of a conversation between Dr. B. and myself, that is truly surprising. Dr. B. represents that he proposed to me a reference of the difficulties in Knox College, to arbitrators; but that 'such an effort at an accommodation of differences *was wholly objected to and refused*, both by Dr. P. and by Dr. Gale.' Dr. B. then adds, as an explanation of the ground on which I 'refused such an effort at accommodation,' that 'Dr. P. asserted *that the College belonged to the N. S. Presbyterians, and that they ought to have the entire control of it*.'

I am sorry to be obliged to pronounce these representations *utterly untrue*. The facts are as follows: A few months after President Blanchard, by request of the Board, resigned, Dr. Beecher came to Chicago and delivered a public lecture on the affairs of Knox College, which abounded in bitter denunciations of the majority of the Board, and of Dr. Gale in particular. This lecture I heard. On the next day after its delivery Dr. B. called on me, and introduced the subject of his lecture, laboring, as I thought, under great mental excitement. He asked what I would think of a reference of the difficulties in the College to arbitrators, with a view to some accommodation of differences. I replied, that I thought his lecture was a very unfortunate preparation for such an accommodation, adding, that the College was wholly under the control of its legally constituted Board of Trust, and that it appeared to me that we in Chicago would be guilty of impertinence in attempting to interfere with its affairs, unless the Board should request our counsel or interposition. This is the substance of all that I said on that point, and Dr. B. knows it perfectly well. After that point was passed in the conversation, I remarked, that I did not think it possible to maintain an exact balance in a Board of College Trustees between two religious denominations, and that if one denomination must have a majority, it should be that one which had done the most to found the institution, as was very properly true in the case of Beloit College, on the Congregational side. I added that, as I understood the facts, the Presbyterians would be entitled, on this principle, to *a majority* in the Board of Knox College. At the same time I said, and repeated the remark, that *no one, so far as I knew, wished that the Presbyterians should have 'the entire control' of the College; that the Congregationalists ought to be liberally represented in the Board*, etc. But I reminded Dr. B. that the Congregationalists had, as yet, more Trustees than the Presbyterians, after all the noise that had been made about the revolutionizing of the College.

I am confident that the statements which I now make are correct, both from my own distinct recollection and from the confirmatory recollection of another person who was present. I can only account for Dr. Beecher's *egregious errors* in the 'testimony' which he has given touching this matter, by attributing them to his extraordinary mental excitement, which must have led to some strange confusion in his thoughts and impressions. It may be proper to add here, that I know of no man in our Church who desires or would consent to the exclusion of Congregationalists from participation in the government of Knox College or of any other Institution which has been established in any measure on the 'co-operative' principle. I have known Rev. W. H. Spencer intimately for many years, and I am sure that he entertains no such views or feelings as have been attributed to him by Rev. L. H. Parker. Our experience has led us to doubt the expediency of establishing any *new* Institutions on the co-operative basis. But we are for keeping all engagements, already made, in good faith.

Very truly yours,

Chicago, Aug. 1, 1859." R. W. Patterson.

This letter of Dr. Patterson was written last summer. The Report of the Committee had then been doing its work of misrepresenting him for more than two months. No word, however, had come from Dr. Beecher correcting or in any way modifying the statement ascribed to him in that Report. No such word has yet come from him, so as to reach the public ear. That, of course, could not be expected of him if he actually made the statement which the Committee ascribe to him. But now mark what follows: In October last, the Synod of Peoria met in Galesburg, and then Dr. Patterson had an opportunity of meeting Dr. Beecher face to face, and of inquiring of him on what grounds he had made such a statement concerning him. The results of that interview will be seen in the following letter:

"REV. J. W. BAILEY: *Dear Brother*—I have recently had an interview with Dr. Beecher. He assures me that the document put forth as his 'testimony,' was never submitted to his inspection, or read to him, before its publication; and that *he never intended to make such statements as it attributes to him.* As I understand him, he and I do not differ much as to the substance of his former conversation or conversations with me respecting Knox College. So much the worse for the *framers* of the document which appears in the pamphlet as Dr. Beecher's testimony.

Yours truly,

CHICAGO, Nov. 1, 1859." R. W. PATTERSON.

So much for the "indubitable facts" contained in the Report drawn up by Rev. W. W. Patton, signed as true by himself and the other members of the Committee associated with him, and adopted and published by the "unanimous" vote of the whole Congregational General Association of Illinois and scattered over the whole country!

14. It would have been most grateful to my feelings had the Report which I am examining permitted me to close my work without any special statements respecting Rev. Edward Beecher, D. D. The Committee, however, have not left me the privilege of remaining entirely silent concerning him, unless, indeed, I consent to leave some important interests of the College to suffer through their extravagant laudation of him for his open and long-continued warfare upon it. The Committee have not been content to assert their belief in his good intentions while he was engaged two years ago in breathing out threatenings and slaughter against the majority of the College Board and all their supporters, but they have, with evident relish for such work as his, pronounced his whole course of personal denunciations "*a defense* of the highest interests of the College and community—yea, of religion and morality." This Committee are of the opinion that "the spirit displayed by Dr. Beecher in his statements and arguments" against the College Board

" was *eminently* Christian." They have fully sanctioned all that he has written against the College. Dr. Beecher has also re-affirmed all his former statements, and renewed all his denunciations, by voting in the Association for the Report of the Committee. He thus virtually challenges criticism.

Dr. Beecher came to Galesburg about five years ago, and took charge of a new Church just organized for him—the "First Congregational Church of Galesburg." He has never been connected with Knox College in any manner, either as a member of its Faculty or its Board of Trustees. His public championship of Mr. Blanchard and the Congregational minority of the Board, in 1857, was wholly voluntary. He was a "passer by" and "meddled with strife not belonging to him," and I apprehend has had abundant reason since then to believe in the truth of the Proverb which announces the unfortunate results of such intermeddling: (Prov. 26 : 17.)

He was not content to discuss principles and questions of policy, but he set himself resolutely to the work of *damaging the character* of every man in the Board who voted for the resignation of Mr. Blanchard. After the removal of Mr. Blanchard, the Board appointed Rev. Mr. Gale to visit the East and secure a candidate for the office of President. Before he reached New York City, Dr. Beecher sent a communication to the *Independent*, which was published, warning the public not to place confidence in Mr. Gale, whose conduct in removing Mr. Blanchard, he charged as "unwise, dishonorable and unjust." He aimed to prevent the success of Mr. Gale's mission by a distinct announcement, that any one who should consent to become President of the College, would "involve himself in a conflict with the moral sense of the whole body of students and the community in Galesburg." He represented his views as those that were shared by "a very large majority of the entire community" in this place.

How truly he represented the community here may be gathered from the fact, that the four leading Evangelical Pastors of this place, representing as many different denominations, immediately sent to the Eastern papers a card, in which they declared that Dr. Beecher's statement in the *Independent* was *not true* of themselves, nor, as they believed, of any considerable portion of their fellow-citizens. Dr. Beecher, not content with this attack upon Mr. Gale, while he was abroad upon a mission for the College, next prepared a long and labored document, in which the majority of the College Board, and

Mr. Gale in particular, were denounced in such terms as I trust only Dr. Beecher knows how to use. His address was published and scattered wide-spread through the land. The secret motive of all his violence may be guessed from the following sentences in his address: "President Blanchard, by resigning his office, of course ceased to be a Trustee; and this act destroyed the *balance of power*, and by the substitution of a Presbyterian President, would give the College wholly into the hands of Presbyterians." "It was simply a proposition that President Blanchard and the Congregationalists should lose all power, and that Mr. Gale and the Presbyterians should gain all power in the Institution." The awful spectre that so frightened him was a "Presbyterian President." Twelve Congregationalists, including the President, and nine New School Presbyterians constituted a very equitable "balance of power." The substitution of a "Presbyterian President" was a jarring of the "balance" which too greatly shocked the "moral sensibilities" of the author of the "Conflict of Ages." The reader may infer the character of his address from the impressions produced by it upon those who heard it. It was first delivered to an audience of nearly a thousand persons in Galesburg. During the two hours spent in its delivery there was no token of approval, from first to last, from that great assembly. On the contrary, many a man there hung his head with sorrow at such an address from such a man. When the address was ended there was no demonstration in its favor. But when a son of Mr. Gale arose, and in behalf of his father, who was yet absent for the College, denounced the address as false and slanderous, then almost the whole assembly burst forth in long continued applause. When quiet was restored, a friend of Dr. Beecher moved that the audience return him a vote of thanks for his address, which motion was not even put to vote, but was substituted by a motion to adjourn, which was carried by a very large majority. In this manner did a Galesburg audience receive this "eminently Christian" address.

Dr. Beecher next went to Chicago, to deliver the same address, determined to make the world acquainted with the "moral assassination" committed by the majority of the Board of Knox College. Whether his address appeared to be at all personal and injurious to the character of those whom he opposed, may be gathered from the letter of Rev. Dr. Patterson already quoted, and also from the following remarks made by the editor of the *North-Western Christian Advocate*, in that paper, under date of August 5, 1857:

"We were a little surprised and humbled that this address, before a public audience, should be made up so largely of *personal* matters. In listening to Dr. Beecher's address one would be led to suppose that the parties whose conduct he described were ignorant of the *first principles* of New Testament religion. Nor would we conclude that the standard of civilization and morality was very elevated. These disclosures are indeed painful, nor can we admire Dr. Beecher's taste in thus consenting to publish them from the house-top."

This is the impression produced by the address upon the mind of a stranger, concerning the majority of the Board of Knox College, of whom some were Presbyterian ministers, some were members of Presbyterian, Baptist and Episcopal churches, one was an ex-member of Congress, another was one of the most eminent lawyers in the State, and all were gentlemen of much more than ordinary intelligence and worth.

Dr. Beecher delivered his address in several of the towns of Northern Illinois with results most unfortunate to his own reputation. Even when men did not doubt the truth of his story, it was a question which they could not answer, why *he* should go retailing such matters through the pulpits of the State? That question has not been satisfactorily answered to this day.

He went also to Quincy, and rehearsed the address in a Congregational Church in that city. Among his hearers was the Honorable O. H. Browning, who resides in Quincy, a member of the Board, and one, in Dr. Beecher's opinion, next in moral depravity to Mr. Gale. The sagacious Doctor, knowing his auditor, heroically suppressed, as he admitted afterward, those sentences in his address that were most offensively personal concerning Mr. Browning, which he had delivered everywhere else. When his address was ended, however, the friends of Mr. Browning requested the audience to remain to hear him in reply. But Dr. Beecher and his friends took counsel together, and decided that it would not be wise to allow Mr. Browning to reply, and so they refused the use of the house for that purpose, and the audience were compelled to retire. The pastor of that church, who had lent his pulpit to Dr. Beecher to assail the Board, and who refused even the floor of the house to Mr. Browning, a Trustee of the College, for a reply, was one of the Congregational members of the College Board. The impression produced by the address in Quincy will be gathered from the following quotations from the *Daily Republican* of that city. In speaking of it, the editor says:

"We think it is in bad taste to carry this matter before the uninterested public, and stir up a *bitter* controversy between denominations when it can do no good whatever. Who is President Blanchard, that he should create such petty disturbances? What is Knox College, that we should have its affairs retailed to us through the press and from the pulpit, *in a manner to create unhappy feeling*, where nothing but kindness and calmness should exist? Among those who seem to be particularly exercised about the action of the Trustees, is Rev. Dr. Beecher, of Galesburg, who is now perambulating the State, *stirring up this feeling* in the churches. Last evening he addressed our citizens at the Center Church, on the subject of the difficulty, and in defense of President Blanchard. In the course of his remarks, we are told, he invited an answer, but when he got through, that privilege was refused the friends of the Trustees of Knox College. We look upon this discussion as one calculated to do no manner of good. Let it be settled quietly at home. Do not bring it here to fret and torment our people, and give the irreligious occasion for their *scoffing* and *derisive* comments."

The same paper contained a communication from a leading citizen of Quincy, who spoke of the address as having charged Dr. Gale "with deception, and malice, and great wickedness." "Is there any man," asks that writer, "not absolutely dead to every sentiment of justice and honor, that does not condemn this lending of a church for the purpose of *defaming* a minister and then refusing it for his defense?" "If Professor Gale be guilty of the things charged upon him last evening, he is liable, on conviction before his Presbytery, *to be deposed from the ministry.*"

I have stated enough to show that wherever Dr. Beecher delivered his address, he shocked the sensibilities of his hearers by the violence of his denunciations of the College Board, and of Mr. Gale in particular. Everywhere he gave the impression, either that he was himself enraged beyond all self-control, or else that those whom he denounced were men of much more than common depravity. To believe Dr. Beecher would require every one, in his own language, "utterly to abhor, repudiate and condemn" the majority of the Trustees of Knox College.

And what other impression could be produced by an address in which such language as the following abounds: "Moral degradation and the anger of God," if the Trustees are not *resisted.* "There is no one thing upon which God looks with more indignation than upon a low and torpid state of the moral sensibility which can see and tolerate ATROCIOUS acts of *dishonor* and *injustice* without remonstrance or rebuke, and continue to *associate* and co-operate with their authors, as if the performance of such deeds, unrepented of, were not deserving of *disgrace and infamy.*" Will the reader think for a moment what must have been the state of mind of this distinguished clergyman, when he could characterise the action of the Trustees, in merely requesting a man, with whom they were not satisfied, to resign, as " atrocious acts of dishonor and injustice?" Was that word " atrocious " when applied to such men " eminently Christian?" Was it no assault upon them to go through the pulpits of the State and into the public press, and declare that they were " deserving of disgrace and infamy?"

Dr. Beecher sweeps all the sympathizers of the College Board to a common destruction with the Trustees. " They," he says, " who can coolly look on and see *atrocious* deeds," by which he means the removal of Mr. Blanchard, and nothing else, " without rebuke and even with pleasure, are totally *rotten and corrupt.* Without the poor excuse of temptation, and from their own *inherent baseness and corruption,* they take pleasure in evil for its own sake." This language, when uttered in plain English, refers to all Presbyterians, Episcopalians, Baptists, and others who think Mr. Blanchard was wisely and righteously removed from office by their representatives in the Board. " Now these men," the Trustees, " have put us in a position in which we are bound utterly to abhor, rebuke, and *resist* their deeds, or else *sink* to their moral level and *fall beneath* the wrath of God." The reader will bear in mind that all these Trustees, of whom Dr. Beecher speaks, except two, are members of evangelical churches—two of them are ministers of the Gospel. But although they were Christian brethren, yet he never wearied of denunciation against them. " If there be anything that God abhors, it must be such injustice as this "—the vote to request Mr. Blanchard to resign! " If this is not *moral assassination,* I know not what is." It was actuated by " enmity, hatred and *malignant* revenge." " A state of society in which such things can be done without rebuke and abhorrence would reduce us to the *lowest grade* of moral degradation, and expose us to the righteous judgments of God." The address contains several columns of matter directed especially against Mr. Gale. Dr. Beecher finds even himself, however, exhausted on this point at last, and thus magnanimously disposes of his victim: "But enough—the subject is too painful and humiliating to pursue! I leave Mr. Gale to the just judgment of God!"

Dr. Beecher seemed to fear that he might not carry his hearers with him in his opposition to the Board, and so he resorted to "the terrors of the law" for assistance: "Has the fear of man," he exclaims, "gained so portentous an ascendancy and risen to a height *so impious* and heaven-daring that men quiver like an aspen before human combinations and plottings, and are not afraid of the withering and blasting curse of Almighty God?" "What would God think of such a base and cowardly indifference to wrong?" "Would not his curse rest upon us?" That is, if the people should be willing to allow a Presbyterian to become President of the College!

These are but a few specimens of that address—and my whole soul loathes the rehearsal of even these few! Is it any wonder that a Galesburg audience of a thousand persons listened to that address in silent amazement, and then overwhelmed with applause the man who arose and told Dr. Beecher to his face that it was false and slanderous? Do we wonder that they refused it the very cheap praise of a vote of thanks? Do we wonder that Doctor Beecher has never recovered and never will recover in this community, from the damaging effect of his own document?

Yet this address was only the beginning of a warfare which he carried on during the summer and autumn of 1857, after the removal of Mr. Blanchard. Week after week witnessed his articles in the newspapers published in Galesburg. His aim was to create here, if possible, a prejudice against the College Board and against Presbyterianism so great that no "Presbyterian President" would be willing to trust himself in our midst. The same spirit pervaded these later writings which had pervaded the address. In one of them Dr. Beecher says: "the majority in removing Mr. Blanchard can no more be defended than they could if they had *poisoned or stabbed* him." And yet Dr. Beecher had before that time declared his opinion that Mr. Blanchard was not a proper man to be President of the College. In another he speaks of the Trustees as exhibiting a "spirit malignant and revengeful." In a third they are represented as seeking "to gratify personal hatred and revenge and sectarian bigotry." A statement eminating from the majority is said by him to be the "obvious offspring of malignant hatred and revenge." The English language, fortunately, is not fertile in terms adapted to express so much wrath as Dr. Beecher had in his heart at that time. Its vocabulary furnished him with a few such terms as "atrocious acts, malignity, hatred and revenge"—but they have no equivalent synonymes. Hence he could do no better than repeat the same language over and over again. Yet Dr. Beecher asserts—and this Committee assert—and the General Association assert, that all this was in no manner a "personal assault," either upon Mr. Gale or upon the College Board, but on the contrary was in spirit and in diction "eminently Christian." They free him from the charge of a "personal attack upon Mr. Gale" by saying that "the criticisms which he passed were upon Dr. Gale as a public man and not as a private individual." Scholastic Committee! If Dr. Gale as "a public man" has been guilty of "atrocious acts of dishonor," guided by a spirit full of "malignity and revenge," and is "deserving of disgrace and infamy," what remains worth saving of the "private individual" of the same name?

On the 10th day of September, 1857, the Presbytery of Peoria and Knox met in Galesburg. Dr. Beecher had then been engaged two months in pouring out his wrath against those who had removed Mr. Blanchard, and against all who approved their action. Of those members of the majority of the College Board who were Presbyterians, nearly all were connected with the Churches of this Presbytery. The assault of Dr. Beecher was thus an assault upon this body of such a character that they could not be indifferent to it. Moreover, there was not probably in all the Churches of that Presbytery a member who did not feel that the removal of Mr. Blanchard was a wise and righteous act. Their objection to him was not grounded upon the fact that he was a Congregationalist, but upon strong personal objections to him as a man. They approved fully the action of the Board in removing him from his office. Yet Dr. Beecher had hurled maledictions, not only against the Board, but against all who sustained them in their action. He had even gone so far as to assert that those who approved of their action were more guilty than the members of the Board by whom the action had been taken. He had characterized the action of the Board as an "atrocious act of dishonor and injustice," and then immediately added, "God even makes it a higher grade of guilt to take pleasure in those who perform *atrocious* deeds than to do them." "Those who can coolly look on and see *atrocious* deeds, without rebuke and even with pleasure, are *totally rotten and corrupt*."

When Dr. Beecher uttered these sentences through the principal cities of the State *he knew to whom they applied.* They were uttered *with special reference* to the Presbyterian supporters of the College Board.

Under these circumstances, that Presbytery met. They spent the principal part of two days in a calm and careful inquiry into the facts of the case, and then adopted the paper of which the Committee so bitterly complain. In that paper, they took the following action:

"The Presbytery have noticed with great grief, the violent, personal assaults which have been made by the Rev. Edward Beecher, in the public papers, and also in public addresses, upon the Rev. G. W. Gale, who is a member of this body. We regard the assault, in manner and in spirit, as an open violation of the law of Christ, as to the treatment of Christian brethren. Whatever may have been his own opinion concerning the correctness of the charges he has made, it is certain that he has not pursued the course prescribed in the New Testament, toward an erring brother. In view of the fact, that these very grave charges have been brought against Mr. Gale, without any inquiry from him as to their correctness, or any effort to lead him to a proper acknowledgment of them if correct, and that *very extraordinary efforts* have been made to extend the knowledge of them, far and wide over our whole land, we are compelled to say that, until the Rev. Edward Beecher *shall undo the wrong* he has committed in this matter, we must, as a Presbytery, regard him *as unworthy of our confidence and Christian courtesy as a minister of the Gospel.*"

Could that Presbytery have retained its own self-respect, and not have done what it did? Could they have asked into their pulpits, and invited to share in their deliberations as a Presbytery, a man who had published them to the whole world as "totally rotten and corrupt?" Yet, Dr. Beecher complains of this action as tending to damage his Christian standing throughout the country. Of course it does—and just so long as he continues to vindicate his conduct, and thus compel that Presbytery to hold him where they now do, he must expect to suffer more and more damage from that action. He has been invited again and again to meet the Presbytery and explain his conduct if he could, so as to allow them to recall their action against him. But he refuses to do it. He must rest assured, that just so long as he continues to be "joined to his idols," just so long will this Presbytery "let him alone." A most unhappy affair this is, but the whole responsibility of it rests entirely upon Dr. Beecher. The Committee, in their Report, ask with an exultant tone, "Did the Presbytery think that *their* mere assertion would destroy the reputation of Edward Beecher?" To this question I reply that the Presbytery had no ambition to rival Dr. Beecher in the work of destroying reputations. They were and are content to leave him alone in his glory, so far as that work is concerned. But not even "the reputation of Edward Beecher!" can deliver him from the crushing weight of that action of Presbytery, so calm and so just, until "he shall undo the wrong" which he has committed.

15. The Committee have labored very earnestly to prove that Dr. Gale has been guilty of many "inaccuracies and self-contradictions" in the statements which he has made at different times, concerning the College. Their efforts to destroy public confidence in his statements show very clearly that they regard him as an important witness. He originated the Plan which resulted in founding Knox College. He has been here, closely connected with it, from the beginning of its history. He is better acquainted with all that history than any other man. Hence, his testimony will have great weight with the public, unless in some way its force can be weakened. This the Committee have worked hard to do. Whether this effort on their part, toward a man who has done the public so much good service, is magnanimous, I leave that public to judge. However, if Dr. Gale has been as unwise and inconsistent as this Committee represent him, I will offer no apology for him, except merely to remark that the men who could publish as truth such a document as this "Rights of Congregationalists," ought to be the last men in the world to taunt him with "inaccuracies and self-contradictions." The public will be able to judge correctly concerning his statements when the following things are taken into account:

First, then, it is not denied that, in a few instances, Dr. Gale has been inaccurate in some of his statements. But these inaccuracies are of trifling importance, and do not relate in any case to the main fact involved. They are confined wholly to details and matters of minor moment. They are just such inaccuracies as almost every man would fall into, who related matters which had occurred many years before, without first consulting documents. As an instance of this kind, over which the Committee make quite an ado, Mr. Gale stated in one of his published articles, that Mr. Simmons had started to go West on his own business, before he was appointed on the Purchasing Committee; when the truth was, as Mr. Simmons testifies, he was notified of his appointment *before* he left his home. This is one of the most noted instances of actual inaccuracy pointed out by the Committee! "*Ridiculus mus!*"

Again, it is admitted here that Mr. Gale has sometimes stated facts in general terms, and also amounts in round numbers, which were either a little more or a little less than the exact fact, although true in substance. As a marked instance of this sort of general statement noticed by the Committee, Mr. Gale once wrote, a year and a half ago, that "the names of Simmons and Tompkins were *not* inserted in the title to the land" bought by the Purchasing Committee; when the truth was, that the name of Simmons, but not of Tompkins, was inserted in the deeds for the 410 acres of cultivated and timber land first bought, but in no others. More than 10,000 acres were bought afterward, in the deeds for which, neither of their names appeared. Mr. Gale's reputation will probably survive that "inaccuracy" which appeared so great in the eyes of the Committee that they devote to it one entire article, under the capital letter "K" in their Appendix. But now notice this, that the Committee, after showing that Mr. Simmons' name *did* appear in the deeds for 410 acres, then leave the public to draw the broad inference that his name is found in the deeds for all the other 10,000 acres! Who was most "inaccurate" in this matter?

Again, it must be borne in mind, that much of the pretended "inaccuracy" of Mr. Gale consists in the mere fact that his statements *do not agree with those of the Committee*. This Committee "investigated" so thoroughly all the points involved in their Report, and proved them so clearly, by comparing them "paragraph by paragraph with the evidence sustaining each position," that any man whose statement differs from theirs is, of course, "inaccurate." I can say nothing in defense of Mr. Gale, on this charge. The Committee will find him "inaccurate" beyond all hope of remedy, if they make their Report the standard of truth.

But once again, it is a serious fact that the most important errors charged against Mr. Gale, result wholly from a *studied perversion* of his language, whether by the Committee, or by some one else for them, I do not say. For instance, when Mr. Gale declares the fact that the Subscribers were not all prepared to pay their subscriptions at the time the Purchasing Committee were sent out, the subscriptions not yet being due, and that therefore he and Mr. Ferris borrowed at the bank $10,000, the Committee so pervert this clear statement of the exact truth as to make Mr. Gale prove that those Subscribers *never paid* their subscription! On pp. 58 and 59 of the Report, occur several just such instances as the above. I cannot be persuaded that the man who drew up that Appendix was ignorant of the fact that he was making Mr. Gale prove the very opposite of what he has always explicitly claimed to be true. The statement of Mr. Gale was clear enough. It was possible to pervert it, and accordingly it was perverted. As it is not my object to answer every charge of this kind of inaccuracy brought against Mr. Gale, but only to indicate where the answer may be found in all these cases, I will leave this remarkable Report without further examination. The reader must feel by this time that the Report is totally unworthy of confidence. The men who drew it up never investigated, as they were required to do, and as the public have supposed was done, the great questions which they have nevertheless ventured to answer so positively. The materials of that Report were prepared for them when they came to Galesburg. While here they carefully avoided the office of the College Treasurer and Secretary, where they could have found documentary evidence for every important point to be determined. They preferred rather to collect here and there such random statements of interested parties as could be used to prove a conclusion already adopted. These materials they wove into a Report which has been scattered through all the West and the East, wherever it could possibly do injury to Knox College.

And now I ask this Committee, what they will do with their Report? Will they continue to circulate it as they have done thus far, with all its errors, to perpetuate the wrong against the College which has already been wrought by it? The Committee cannot free themselves from responsibility in this matter. They have wronged the College—undesignedly, "through ignorance," I trust. But now, when they read the College records—when they see the facts contained in the books of its Treasury—when they hear the voice of its founders, will they disregard all this, and still allow their Report to go as though it were true? They cannot deny the truth and force of the documents published in this pamphlet. If they think they are not correct, or do not correctly represent the facts of the case, they are bound to show it by examining those documents for themselves. The Secretary and Treasurer of the College would gladly have given them the opportunity to do this when they were in Galesburg. They will as gladly give them this opportunity hereafter if they desire it. Those officers certify that the documents here published are correctly given, and do present the true history of the College. It is not, therefore, a question of judgment, or of veracity, between me and the Committee. The question lies between the Committee, and the College and its founders. If the College records and other documents are not correct, and if the founders of the College are mistaken concerning themselves, the Committee must show it; or else they must not only recall their Report, but also inform the public that they were mistaken, and that the Report is not true. If the Committee mean to deal honestly with the College they must do this. If they mean to deal honestly with their own denomination and with the public, they must do this. The College, the Church, and the whole public, will turn their eyes upon this Committee to see what they will do.

Knox College was founded by wise and good men, who consecrated it to the interests of sound learning, and of manly culture in the service of " Christ and the Church." They founded it in order that it might aid in establishing the kingdom of Christ among men. To accomplish this noble mission it must be administered with wisdom and justice and the highest Christian principle. Its founders were not ignorant of this fact, nor were they indifferent to it. That it might be directed always toward the end for which it had been established, they expected and intended that it would be controlled mainly by men belonging, like themselves, to the Presbyterian Church. By this, however, they did not mean to subject it to any " ecclesiastical " control, nor did they mean that it was to be in any sense a " sectarian " College. No denomination, as such, was ever to have any voice in its control. It was to be used, not to build up a sect, but to educate youth, of every and any sect. It was to be a College for the benefit of the whole Church and the whole State. That it may become such a College, it must be elevated above the reach of sectarian and denominational strife. Its Board must not be the scene of angry struggles between jarring sectaries for party pre-eminence. There must be no such equipoise of rival sects as to cause the Board to hesitate to appoint any evangelic man to its corps of instructors, who is exactly qualified for the post, from any fear that his weight will be thrown into the one scale or the other, and disturb the " balance." · The word " sect " or " denomination " must not be heard or known in its Board, except merely to keep that

Board true to the Church from which the College sprung, and thus keep the College true to the end for which it was called into existence. This is what its founders intended for Knox College. It was administered true to this principle during its early years. After a time, secretly and steadily, a rival "sect" sprung up within its Board, and, in the hour of its strength, struggled hard to make the College "sectarian." Against this attempt the majority of the Board, men of various denominations, set themselves, resolutely and *righteously*. They were and are determined that Knox College shall be what its founders intended it to be. It will thus be planted upon the same platform as that which has so long given stability and success to our Eastern Colleges. In New England, every College but one, is so under the predominating control of some one denomination, as to lift them above all danger from sectarian strife. In Harvard alone, do we hear the sound of war, and the cause there is the departure from the broad principle which gives peace to all the rest.

Unitarian Congregationalism and Orthodox Congregationalism in New England, although one sprang out of the other, as did Minerva from the brain of Jove, cannot live peacefully together, and cannot harmonize, even in the control of a College. Hence Harvard is the arena of strife. Yale, and Williams, and Amherst, have no such trouble, because Orthodox Congregationalists are in them the supreme power. While human nature remains anywhere near what it is now, no equal division of denominations in a College Board, unaccompanied by strife, will long be possible. Slowly, it may be, but surely one party will gain the permanent ascendancy over the others. In the last number of the *New Englander* is an article headed "Denominational Colleges," by a writer well known as President of one of our Western Colleges. The arguments of that writer, while evidently aimed at some other institution than the one over which he presides, are, nevertheless, like that famous weapon of the warrior of Madagascar, which, when hurled, however far away, is said always to return and *strike* at the very feet of him who hurled it. In that article the writer uses this language : " It is within the memory of men yet not far from the meridian of life, that the thought had scarcely been entertained by any mind, that a College should be in any sense the representative of a sect; or, that such Colleges as Princeton, and Columbia, and Yale, were not suitable for the education of any American youth, whatever might be the religious views of his parents." Leaving the writer to reconcile, if he can, this language with the evident bearing of his whole argument, I desire heartily to commend all that is involved in the reference he has made to the three Colleges named. Those Colleges have long been eminently successful. They have deserved, as they have received abundantly, the confidence and patronage of the public. No discord disturbs the harmony of their operations. And the reason is, that each one is under the controlling influence of members of a single denomination. Princeton is well known as Presbyterian, Columbia as Episcopalian, and Yale as Congregational. We ask only that Knox College may be planted upon that same foundation, which has proved so strong and immovable in the case of Yale and Columbia, and Princeton. Its founders placed it upon exactly such a foundation. There it will be kept by its Board hereafter. That which renders Eastern Colleges stable will give stability to Colleges at the West. And nothing else will.

Knox College is open to all denominations and to all classes alike. It offers to educate a Congregational youth just as fully as it does one who is Presbyterian. And this offer extends to all denominations. Congregationalists complain that they can no longer patronize it—that they are driven from it. How this can be I do not know, unless it be impossible for them to patronize a College not wholly their own. Presbyterian young men find no difficulties of conscience in attending the Congregational Colleges of New England. Why may not a Congregational youth attend a College that is largely controlled, though not wholly, by his own denomination here at the West? Does the partial Presbyterianism of the Board affect the quality of the studies, so that the very same course of instruction, which was of measureless benefit under a Congregational Board, ceases to be valuable when the "sect" loses power? Have our Congregational brethren in Illinois at last come to that? I do not think so. The Congregational body of this State has been misled by a few men, who have wished to avenge themselves upon the College for refusing to be perverted from its original design. They have been persuaded that they have been deprived of all their rights here. They have been led to believe that the College is henceforth to be used for narrow and sectarian ends. All this is false. The narrowness and "sectarianism," that for a few years past were sinking it in the popular esteem throughout the State, are now removed. The College now is devoted to a higher mission than that of merely reflecting the opinions and peculiarities of *one man*. It has a noble endowment, which is becoming more fully available every day. It has a Faculty more in numbers and wiser in experience than it has ever had before; and they are *all of one heart*, and are all devoted to the prosperity of the College. The dividing line of denominations is not known within the sphere of the College Faculty. The College buildings are new and massive structures—an ornament to the city, and an honor to the Institution. The course of studies is the same as that of the first Colleges of New England. Knox College is an honor to the State of Illinois. If Congregationalists cannot patronize such an Institution, the fault is with them and not with the College. The College was founded in prayer—it was consecrated to the good of man—it has secured an endowment by a marvellous providence—it has advanced with rapid strides to the front rank of similar institutions—it has manifestly a noble destiny before it. The sympathies of the people, who dwell on these broad prairies, cannot be turned away from such an institution. ITS PROSPERITY IS THEIR GLORY—ITS ADVERSITY WILL BE THEIR MISFORTUNE. Whoever, therefore, may oppose it, and whatever temporary evils it may suffer, it will still move onward, in unwavering faith in that sublime truth unfolded in those hopeful words—JEHOVAH-JIREH!

Printed in Dunstable, United Kingdom